"Darryl has been a brother in Christ for several years and I have grown to trust in his wisdom and stewardship."

—David Robinson, NBA Hall of Famer, Founder of the Carver Academy

"Darryl's response to God's relentless pursuit will inspire any leader! A must read in today's marketplace!"

—Randy Frazee, Senior Minister Oak Hills Church, author of *The Connecting Church, Making Room for Life, The Christian Life Profile Assessment,* and *Renovation of the Heart Student Edition*

"Today's business world requires innovation and forward thinking. In the midst of the changing environment Darryl reminds us to examine our unique calling. He forces us to think through the seriousness of aligning faith with our work. One of the most practical business and faith books on the market today!"

—John Lee Dumas, Founder and host of Entrepreneur on Fire

"Many years ago I read a book called *The "E" Myth*. It changed my life in a positive way. Yet I have always felt a twinge in referring that book because it has no Christian message. Darryl Lyons has written a Christ-centered book that has tons of practical applicational value but also recognizes our Savior as our true source of all wisdom and purpose. This book will be extremely helpful to all those who are feeling the urge to start a business are at the stage where they have started and are struggling wit how to grow it. Well done Darryl!"

—Buck Jacobs, Chairman and Founder of the C12 (

"*Small Business, Big Pressure* is a timely tool that helps entrepreneurs successfully integrate their faith with every other fiber of their lives. Darryl shows us how effective marketplace ministry is not only an emerging trend, but also why it's here to stay."

—Kary Oberbrunner, CEO of Redeem the Day & Igniting Souls, Author of *Your Secret Name, The Deeper Path,* and *Day Job to Dream Job*

"Darryl's book is exactly the right book at the right time. In an age where common sense isn't common practice anymore, Darryl reminds us that tried & true principles are at all of our disposal; awaiting for our discovery & implementation."

—Richard Rierson, Founder and host of Dose of Leadership Podcast

"As a faith-based entrepreneur, I especially appreciate the approach of *Small Business, Big Pressure*. The content dives deep into key areas of business like profit margin, cash flow, and ratios. But it doesn't stop there. Important topics like hiring, firing and successfully interacting with different personalities are dealt with in a way that's easy to understand and implement. Darryl does a masterful job of sharing business truths that will ultimately lead you to a closer walk with Christ."

—Jevonnah "Lady J" Ellison, Founder of Maximum Potential Academy

"In *Small Business Big Pressure*, author Darryl Lyons presents powerful lessons in "Can-do-ism" for getting on track personally and financially."

—Patty Wyatt, *Girlfriendit Radio*

"This book is written from the entrepreneur's battlefield and delivers a beautiful backhand of perspective, taking your business, leadership, and life to the next level and beyond."

—Mark Minard, CEO/Owner of Dreamshine, Co-Host of Elevating Beyond

"Darryl's personal story is an inspiration and evidence that you can still 'win' in the truest sense of the word despite hardship, hard-knocks, and hard mistakes. He combines his story with common-sense business for the common man that can help anyone achieve uncommon success!"

— Rob Wainner, PhD, Coach 4 Leadership, President and Founder

"In a culture that compartmentalizes our careers, personal integrity, and faith, Darryl's journey proves that integrating these elements yields true success."

—Lee Caple, Founder of Caple Royalty Services

"Darryl is a solid Christian man who deposits his biblical beliefs into action in the most organized business model/practice I have worked with in twenty-five years. I aspire to learn and copy some of his concepts in our own business model."

—Chad Atkins CFP®, CRPC, Co-founder of 360 Wealth Management

"From the outside looking in, it's easy to want to dislike Darryl. He is good looking, athletic, intelligent, humble, a man of principle, very successful, and has a wonderful family. From the inside looking out, as you get to know Darryl, you cannot help to fall in love with him. He has aligned his life according to God's will and he is a living example of God's blessings!"

—John Michael Raimondo, D.C. Founder of Pulmonair

"Darryl is a definitive, proven resource in how to do exceedingly well . . . by doing exceedingly good."

—Chuck Bowen, Founder and Owner of Chuck Bowen Coaching, LLC, TrueBlue Production LLC, and Scott Stearman Productions, LLC

"Darryl's character shines through his pursuit of excellence in each domain of his life."

—Doug Heintz, Co-founder of Home Court America Family Sports & Fitness Center, San Antonio, Texas

"I am consistently impressed and inspired by Darryl's vision, drive, and single-minded focus on results."

—Brian Booker, Founder of ExploreUSA RV Supercenter

"Darryl Lyons has a unique combination of integrity, character, knowledge, and professionalism that not only makes him a role model for our children, but one we should all seek to follow."

"Darryl Lyons is a dynamic entrepreneur that has mastered the ability to take all of the great qualities he possesses as a magnetic, faithful, and compelling individual and inject those invaluable characteristics right into his business, leaving lasting impressions on his team, colleagues, and clients."

""Darryl has the knowledge, experience and wit to express an amazing personal journey to keep you engaged, with deep understanding of how to run a business. He teaches us how to make business possible and how to live out each aspect of our business through our faith. Us entrepreneurs have a gift to build and drive ideas, but we don't always have the gift to lead or manage a business where the rubber hits the ground. Darryl's insights and faith are inspiring and wise for any Business Owner, President or CEO."

As an investor and entrepreneur, Darryl's competence inspires my confidence to make wise, informed decisions."

"Darryl Lyons is a rock-star business leader that successfully blends the values of his faith with the pressures of running a business."

"The title sounds like a business book but it's much more! Filled with nuggets about life, leadership, and finances, this volume will help anyone entrusted with building an organization. I highly recommend it to my fellow vocational ministers or anyone leading in the local church."

"... trustworthy and inspiring leader who serves as an outstanding role model for family, business, and a Christ-centered life."

—Tracey Blackwell, Owner TBlackwell Insurance Group

"Darryl Lyons has been a source of both financial and spiritual wisdom in my life for well over a decade."

—Chad Schapiro, Founder of OurGV Inc.

"I've been in the trenches with Darryl and he's the real deal. If you want to wrestle with your faith alongside a fellow entrepreneur this is a must read book!"

—Andres Gutierrez, Financial Expert and Nationally Syndicated Radio Host

"Entrepreneurs and leaders that desire to live a life of significance and joy often don't know how to get there. This book will propel you to the place of perfect clarity on how to partner with God in finding your calling. Darryl will teach you to start working with God to achieve success and freedom from fear and worry."

—John Ramstead, CPLC, Founder of the Ramstead Group Inc. and host of
Eternal Leadership Podcast

SMALL BUSINESS
BIG
PRESSURE

A Faith-based Approach to Guide the Ambitious Entrepreneur

DARRYL W. LYONS

NEW YORK

SMALL BUSINESS BIG PRESSURE

Readers should be aware that Internet Web sites offered as citations and/or sources for further information may have changed or disappeared between the time this was written and when it is read.

Published in New York, New York, by Morgan James Publishing. Morgan James and The Entrepreneurial Publisher are trademarks of Morgan James, LLC.
www.MorganJamesPublishing.com

The Morgan James Speakers Group can bring authors to your live event. For more information or to book an event visit The Morgan James Speakers Group at www.TheMorganJamesSpeakersGroup.com.

Shelfie

A **free** eBook edition is available with the purchase of this print book.

CLEARLY PRINT YOUR NAME ABOVE IN UPPER CASE

Instructions to claim your free eBook edition:
1. Download the Shelfie app for Android or iOS
2. Write your name in **UPPER CASE** above
3. Use the Shelfie app to submit a photo
4. Download your eBook to any device

ISBN 9781630476519 paperback
ISBN 9781630476526 eBook
Library of Congress Control Number:
2015908195

Cover Design by:
Chris Treccani
www.3dogdesign.net

Interior Design by:
Chris Treccani
www.3dogdesign.net

In an effort to support local communities, raise awareness and funds, Morgan James Publishing donates a percentage of all book sales for the life of each book to Habitat for Humanity Peninsula and Greater Williamsburg.

Get involved today, visit
www.MorganJamesBuilds.com

Habitat
for Humanity®
Peninsula and
Greater Williamsbur
Building Partner

FOR MY CARESSE

CONTENTS

PART 3: DIALOGUE

PART 4: IDENTITY

FOREWORD

I was a business owner for twenty-five years. As a result, I understand all the issues that business owners have to deal with on a daily basis. What I have not seen until the publication of this book, is a book that gives business owners an understanding of what it looks like to run a Christ-centered business. That is why I am excited that the Lord prompted Darryl Lyons to write such a book.

I have known Darryl for a number of years. I have witnessed the Lord move him from being a driven, success-focused businessman to a Christ-centered businessman. I no longer see a man who is driven and motivated by the world's definition of success. Rather, I see a Christ-focused entrepreneur whose greatest desire in business is to honor Christ and to make his business his ministry. As a result, Darryl's employees and his clients are experiencing the transforming life of Christ through him. In addition, God has created a Christ-focused work culture in his business.

That is why whether you are a business owner or an employee; I highly recommend that you read *Small Business Big Pressure*. It will give you fresh new insight on how Christ can live His life through you to transform your business into a place of ministry. You will see how Christ can use your business to transform you, your clients, and fellow employees. Since Darryl includes much of his personal story, you will get a glimpse into how the Lord worked in and through Darryl to produce a Christ-centered workplace.

Therefore, I trust the truths in this book will draw you closer to Christ personally and give you a deeper understanding of what Christ wants to do through your life to produce a Christ-focused workplace.

Bill Loveless
Christ Is Life Ministries

Like any other eleven-year-old boy in the 1980s, my interests included video games, University of Miami Football, and Robocop. My greatest worry in life was if Jose Canseco and Mark McGwire were going to make the All-Star team (boy, they sure fooled me!). Meanwhile, miles away from my small Texas town, Wall Street was on the brink of collapse. Michael Milken collected a rap sheet for hustling junk bonds. Warren Buffett placed a bet on a little insurance company called GEICO. The entire US economy experienced a seismic shift.

Between me and the 1987 savings and loan crisis stood the strongest man I know—my father, Darryl W. Lyons. Having the same name didn't get weird until Bob Newhart came out with a television show about a couple of redneck brothers named Darryl, Darryl, and Larry. Then, when we introduced ourselves together, "Hi, I'm Darryl Senior," "I'm Darryl Junior," I would count in my head, "One, two, three," and boom! We'd get a predictable comedic comment about Larry, Darryl, and his other brother, Darryl.

My dad excelled in life despite lacking a high school diploma. Early childhood for him was tumultuous, and at age sixteen, he was completely on his own. Before he was of legal age to vote, my father found himself looking for work to pay for a roof over his head. Out of desperation, he took whatever employment he could find. He learned very quickly what he needed to do to join the business community. Riding the fast track, he cultivated a sharp business acumen and corporate America came calling. A large fire and safety firm snatched him up and quickly gave him the responsibility equivalent to those with silver hair.

My father became the prototypical 1980s businessman. I loved his fire engine red pickup, big bulky car phone, and his Apple IIe computer. He had a mustache like Burt Reynolds, a Marlboro between his lips, and a sharp suit resting on his athletic physique. My dad's success was reflected in the pile of his uncashed personal payroll checks sitting on the kitchen counter. We were happy. Life was sweet.

In October 1987, as the Texas sun came creeping above the hill country horizon, my father drove to his office, knowing intuitively that the early bird gets the worm. My brother and I sat in the backseat of his truck looking forward to our day of play; our father's mind focused on beating quotas and flexing his managerial muscles.

Just like any other day, my dad parked, walked up to the door, and inserted his key. Only this time, the key didn't trigger the mechanism in the lock. Turning the key the other way couldn't convince the springs and levers to stir the bolt either. My dad picked up his car phone that was connected to an oversized battery pack in his truck, and called the building manager. My brother and I waited, watching expectantly. As it turned out, building management had received instructions from my dad's employer to change the locks during the weekend. So dad called corporate, and corporate responded with, "Darryl, you're fired." Just like that.

Before this day, I had never seen a tear fall from my father's eyes. In my child's mind, I couldn't grasp the magnitude of what had happened. Very quickly, my family atmosphere changed pressure. The way my mom and dad whispered behind closed doors was an omen to the challenges ahead. Children are observant, and I was sneaky-observant. I pretended to play with toys, knowing if I didn't interrupt, I could eavesdrop and overhear the truth in the details.

As a result of the broken dream, school supplies became a luxury and auto insurance was optional. On several occasions, the mortgage was paid from a jar of quarters, nickels, and dimes. Every Christmas, the kids would hope for the best but expect the worst. In a season of transition, I slept on a concrete floor with only a thin layer of Berber carpeting for a mattress. We tried to disguise our financial madness behind the mask of living in a suburban community. When we finally moved into a single-wide trailer, our money struggles were exposed to the world.

Most of the time, being broke only hurt when I knew others knew. Going without didn't pain me as much as little kids saying things like, "At least I can afford a hacky sack." Those comments became more frequent—too frequent. They wounded my identity.

We moved more often than a child would prefer. Pen pal friends faded with time. My senior year of high school, we relocated to a small trailer park in the tiny Texas town of Castroville. Lack of money magnified other existing problems, and my mom and dad fought. They fought a lot. Meantime, my brother, sister, and I were all searching for hope. The key that the door rejected broke our family.

Solely because of that "key," I decided with every fabric of my being that I didn't want this to happen to me again. Lodged in my gut was a desire to defend myself from a useless "key." I cultivated my strategy at a young age; my soul made a promise to my head— you will never work for someone else. You couldn't convince me that my father messed up his onetime shot by getting crossways with corporate. You couldn't convince me the fault of Michael Milken and the savings and loan crisis caused our downfall. You couldn't convince me simple corporate layoffs were the reason for my tears. The nemesis and my enemy was "the key."

Fast-forward to today and the story is the handiwork of God's mystery. My younger sister, Sarah, who shared my experience but with her own set of personal challenges, is an extremely successful artist and entrepreneur. My little brother, Franklin, who navigated his life only slightly differently than Sarah did, ended up with the same outcome. He is a Texas Silicon Valley entrepreneur. Even my father and mother now own their own profitable business. We all have degrees of success in being our own boss. We wouldn't live life any other way. We are living the American Dream.

The life of the entrepreneur comes with some "attaboys" if done the right way. My small business was recognized by the *San Antonio Business Journal* as one of "The Best Places to Work" and one of "The Fastest Growing Companies" in the community. We keep growing year after year and we do it with a team that loves showing up on Monday mornings. Success is difficult in any community but it is especially hard with stiff competition in the seventh largest city in the country.

More important than the accolades, I have counseled hundreds of business owners on how to make fundamental yet serious business decisions impacting many lives. Many business owners suppress daily pressures, become overwhelmed by worry, and experience a messy mind of decisions. If I assist an entrepreneur in the transformation from chaos to living an abundant small business life, everyone wins. The owner finds rest. The secretary doesn't have to pay rent from a jar of change. Kids enjoy Christmas. The business excels. I get goose bumps on my goose bumps collaborating with a fellow business owner who lives the American Dream.

ACKNOWLEDGEMENTS

Thank you, Lord, for not giving up on me.

Thank you to my wife, Caresse, and our children, Luke, Claire, Noelle, and Lucy. Your smiles make me stronger. Mom and Dad, you inspire me every day. Thank you to my brother, Franklin, and his wife, Stephanie. Thank you to my sister, Sarah. To my in-laws/friends, Duane and Lou, your love and your cooking keep me going.

I love my PAX team. You guys take care of business! Thank you to Joseph and Stacey Schuetze for your years of supporting all of my crazy ambitions.

Thank you to those whose creativity influenced the production of this book: CrossBooks Publishing, Michelle Booth, Janise Brooks, Andres Gutierrez, Fermin Hernandez, Bill Loveless, Sergio Luna and the Rojo 032 Team, Mike Sharrow, Robert Vogel, Rob Wainner, and Roger Whitney.

INTRODUCTION

1 DESTINATION   DOLLARS 2

Small Business
Owner

4 IDENTITY   DIALOGUE 3

The American Dream is real. A business owner kicks off a new year with only imagination limiting his income potential. He wakes up on Monday and decides if it is going to be a nine-to-five day or a ten-to-two day. No one complains when he shows up a few minutes late. No one mumbles or grumbles when his lunch hour crawls past one o'clock. No one is telling him to wear a suit. Today, he'll wear blue jeans.

Attached to the perks of this "entre-freedom" is a string—the string of responsibility. After hours, the business owner brings home a burden most civil service workers and employees leave at the office: the responsibilities of money and people that bring along gray hair and high blood pressure. The entrepreneur wakes up at midnight with worries of paying bills, and again at three thirty a.m. with troubled thoughts of an employee argument. He just wants to sleep and dream of the so-called "balanced life."

Ideally, the scale measures freedom and responsibility equally. But ultimately, the scale tilts and responsibility becomes heavy. The dream quickly becomes a nightmare. He considers returning to the world of a steady paycheck and a company clock. He reminds himself of the bridge he burned and there's no going back. Motivated by the combination of the love for his family and his own pride, the business owner wakes up early and presses on. He gets his mind over mattress with a crack-of-dawn work ethic. His work pattern is mostly comprised of early mornings, late nights, and weekends. If his schedule isn't full, his mind is. He is worried and tired, but mostly worried. **It doesn't have to be this way.**

The entrepreneur usually associates worry solely as a physical problem that causes stomach ulcers and heart palpitations. Physical problems are fueled by a bad night's rest, lack of a good meal, or a distracted life. Failures, problems, and physical mistakes are normal and natural, and the business owner tries to learn from them. A good business leader files the failures in the memory cabinet and learns from them for the future. But even with the benefit of learning a lesson, physical mistakes can cost the business some money. They might even cost a customer or an employee.

However, it's important for small-business owners to understand the spiritual connection to worry. Physical mistakes typically can be recovered from, whereas spiritual mistakes can destroy a marriage, family, and business. Spiritual brokenness will put the entrepreneur in the corner of a room in the fetal position. Spiritual problems **(worry, pressure, and confusion)** are more common and more powerful than physical mistakes.

I admit, I have an excellent track record of physical mistakes that cost me a few bucks to fix. But my entrepreneurial spiritual problems are not just more expensive, they leave a heavier mark on those around me. So I don't fall victim to the thief of entrepreneurial freedom and peace. I have removed myself from the center of the business and allowed God to take over. My business and my leadership have become dependent on the Founder and Creator of business—God.

As I advised families and businesses for the last several years, I hunted for commonalities that could improve their financial lives. My desire was to find a silver bullet for financial success in small business. After many conversations and homework, I found clues, but never the bullet. Instead, I discovered something even more powerful. I identified a clear, repeatable cycle consistent among every business, from sole proprietorships to complex organizations.

The above diagram references this cycle. Let me spend a minute explaining this consistent small business experience.

First, the entrepreneur has a good idea and a vision of his future. He begins to define the **DESTINATION** of his life, his family, and his business. Then, as he moves toward his destination by selling products and services, cash flow reflects his efforts. As **DOLLARS** fill up the bank account, he can't handle the workload on his own and needs help. He now must hire employees. Quality daily **DIALOGUE** with his employees is key for operating his small business. As he continues to build his team, he needs everyone thinking and behaving as a unified team. The final step requires the owner to create a company **IDENTITY**.

He repeats this process as his business grows, he develops new products, and enters new markets. Lather, rinse, and repeat.

The Problem:

Every time the entrepreneur enters a new phase in the cycle it creates an incredible amount of **pressure** on him. Throughout the cycle, the entrepreneur becomes increasingly **worried** and can't arrange the mess of **confusion**. This chaos is a roadblock to the life he can and should enjoy.

The Process:

The entrepreneur has to give up his control and recognize he is not the epicenter of the small-business cycle. The idea of giving up control requires moment by moment dependence upon the

Creator of the Universe to guide the decision-making process. The trust and dependence someone gives to a surgeon is the same type of trust the entrepreneur needs to give to God. As we put our lives into the hands of a surgeon when we go under the knife, so an entrepreneur puts his life into the hands of God.

The Benefit:

When the entrepreneur allows his business to be centered on God and His infinite attributes, he experiences an abundant life. He transfers the pressure to God. His worry is exchanged for trust. His business strategy becomes clear. He's no longer confused because he gets to access the Author of wisdom. Once blind, now he sees. He only wishes he would have done this sooner.

Hard work and late nights are a prerequisite for any great business, but worry shouldn't be the thief of the abundant life. I am going to convince you that **pressure, worry, and confusion** will only be a passing guest in your house and business. You will not let them stay overnight to steal, kill, and destroy. Your anxiousness will leave and your mind will be clear. A fellow entrepreneur named Paul, as he was preaching to his European colleagues, gave the idea of this unique business clarity in the Bible. Paul said that we need to quit comparing ourselves to other business people and completely transform the way we think. This new approach will transform and renew your mind so you can experience the abundant business life you were meant to experience.

The four sections of this book can be read independently of each other based on the entrepreneur's needs. However, it is worth mentioning that there are two over-arching themes to this book. The first is the practical application of business skills I have personally deployed. This application will give you knowledge, and when coupled with unique business strategies, you will be ready for any business implementation. You will be able to walk through my small business and observe the execution of proven tools. The second theme is the story of my personal entrepreneurial journey of becoming more dependent upon God.

Another important component of this book can be found at the end of each of the four sections. There, you will see a special chapter that gets to the heart of what it means to live an abundant life. The titles of all four of these unique chapters are the same, Dependence. In these sections, I attempt to be vulnerable about my experience and how God is constantly moving me toward a greater dependence on Him through His relentless pursuit of my life. Enjoy.

At the end of each chapter are next steps relative to the discussed topic.

ACTION ITEM:

A series of practical applications ready for you to implement in your business today.

PRAYER:

EACH PRAYER IS STATED NOT AS A "GOD, HELP

ME" PRAYER (SEE HOW THIS WORKED FOR ABRAM

IN GEN. 16.). THIS TYPE OF PRAYER MAY ASSUME

THE ENTREPRENEUR IS THE SOURCE OF PEACE,

BOLDNESS, AND CLARITY. RATHER, EACH PRAYER

IS DESIGNED FOR THE ENTREPRENEUR TO BE

COMPLETELY DEPENDENT ON THE ALMIGHTY

CREATOR AS THE SOURCE.

PART 1: DESTINATION

1

DEFINING THE DESTINATION

Despite his unique intelligence, Albert Einstein had a reputation of being absent minded. There is a story that on one particularly cold winter day, Einstein elected to travel by train from one industrial town to the next. Prior to stepping on the locomotive, a young conductor requested Einstein's ticket. He frantically scrambled in search of the boarding pass. Reaching into his jacket and pant pockets, and even in the cuff of his pant legs. His ticket was lost. Einstein's haircut kept him from remaining anonymous. "Mr. Einstein, there is no need to fret about your ticket," the conductor said. "I know who you are. Feel free to come on board." The conductor courteously opened his hand to show him the way to the entrance.

Einstein settled in a dimly lit seat by himself in the back as he continued to search for the lost ticket. The conductor, recognizing the discomfort Einstein was experiencing, briskly walked over and kindly, yet directly, explained to Einstein, "Don't be concerned about the ticket Mr. Einstein. My train is your train. No ticket necessary." Einstein paused, breathed, and looked up from his seat. In his thick German accent, he replied, "Young man, I don't need the ticket to board the train, I need the ticket to know where I am going."

The story reflects the reality of an entrepreneur. Somewhere along the way, Mr. Einstein's mind became messy with ideas and strategy, and thus lost sight of his destination. Likewise, the entrepreneur's mind gets hazy. He stands in the middle of a cornfield blanketed by fog and mist. He moves because being paralyzed means death, but he still doesn't know where he's going. Stress, pressure, and worry keep his mind cloudy. His work ethic has his blood circulating and his heart beating but there is no destination in sight. He's only manufacturing crop circles.

For the entrepreneur standing in the foggy cornfield and **knowing the destination,** is like having a ladder and a flashlight. Defining the destination, by creating a company mission, vision, and goals, gets him out of the fog. These three components provide clarity to the entrepreneur and to the team. Often, the entrepreneur has an idea of his destination lodged deep in his gut. However, he needs to step aside from the push of daily demands and exercise the powerful process of writing down the future. This process inscribes the vision on his consciousness. The two major benefits of defining the destination are (1) Focus and (2) Motivation.

Focus

Mr. Einstein was a genius of the past, so let's consider icons and geniuses of the present. What do Warren Buffett and Bill Gates, Sr. have to say about defining a destination? One evening as the sun rested on the waters, the two enjoyed dinner with friends. I would imagine lobster, the most experienced wait-staff, and wine that is designed to be smelled before being tasted. Buffett would request a Cherry Coke. A few of the politicians, judges, and businessmen attending the dinner would do the same only to patronize Mr. Buffett.

After a few drinks, one member of the group had the confidence to pose a question to the table: *What factor did they feel was the most important element that got them to where they were in life?* Pause. No one wanted to misstep.

After deliberation, Buffett and Gates concurred, it was focus. The specific type of focus they were referring to was the type that sparks "intensity." Entrepreneurs desire intensity but get sidetracked because of a lack or complete loss of focus. It only requires a little entrepreneurial effort to climb the ladder with a flashlight in hand, get the team focused, and enjoy the return of intensity.

Motivation

When the entrepreneur climbs the ladder and sees above the cornfield, he then becomes motivated. He's motivated to continue to place bets and work late because he is convinced the destination is bliss. An entrepreneur who has a well-defined destination is inspired knowing one day he will be able to take time off and enjoy a steak dinner. But more importantly, he's motivated to change the lives in his community through his company.

The team also experiences a new kind of motivation. Employees can only be motivated by a paycheck for so long. They often dread Mondays and celebrate TGIF a little too much. The benefits package isn't a motivator; it's only a buffer between them and Monster.com. If the entrepreneur puts a little more in the 401k, gratefulness doesn't transcend having to deal with an angry customer. However, when the entrepreneur stands on the ladder and lights the way to the destination, the team will experience a new kind of motivation. The team is transformed from a collective group of people doing a job to a crusade for positive change. Entrepreneurs would rather lead a crusade than individual employees. Likewise, employees would rather follow a crusade than a boss.

In this section, we will talk about how to define the destination and how to cast vision for your team. We will climb the ladder of a mission statement and a vision statement. Then, we will develop well-thought-out goals. Next, I'll hand you a few flashlights that will keep you and your team focused. Lastly, we'll qualify how critical it is for the entrepreneur to be 100 percent dependent on God while defining the destination.

ACTION ITEM

Answer the following question: Can I confidently articulate my company vision?

PRAYER

LORD, MY MIND IS STUCK IN THE FOG AND I'M

CONFUSED. FRANKLY, I DON'T KNOW WHERE I AM

GOING. BE MY LIGHT.

2

MISSION STATEMENT

The mission statement answers the question: Why does the company exist?

Specifically, a mission statement formula is:

What the company does +

Who the company does it for =

Mission statement

(sometimes it includes: + How the company does it).

A simple way to start a mission statement process is to use the phrase, *"We exist to..."* This phrase helps shape the entrepreneur's mind-set for creating a powerful mission statement. The mission statement defines the organization's purpose, so every word must be deliberate. The entrepreneur can keep the phrase *"We exist to"* in the mission statement or he can remove it while he wordsmiths. The revision might make the statement feel more authentic but it takes time and a few rounds of, *"No, that doesn't sound right."* When it is completed, the mission statement should only be one strong, concise sentence. Take out the fluff and shoot it straight. Below are three examples of powerful mission statements:

"Use our pioneering spirit to responsibly deliver energy to the world."

—Conoco Phillips[1]

"To bring inspiration and innovation to every athlete in the world."

—Nike[2]

"To bring generational change to Middle America through a process of independent advice and principled leadership."
—PAX Financial Group, LLC

The most valuable benefit of a mission statement is that it becomes a filter. The mission statement gives a company a sense of order and guides the decision-making process. Every purchase decision and project initiative must be filtered through the mission statement. For example, our company focuses on middle-class America, not the affluent. We drew a line in the sand when we created this mission. This means if "top-of-the-line," "cutting edge," "innovative" software packages that cater to the elite are dangling in front of us, we don't take the bait. They're not for us. This filtering process keeps us focused, not distracted by dead-end routes found in the corn maze.

A young lady I know had a mission statement—my mom. Growing up, my mom was routinely exposed to family instability. Unfortunately, the family challenges were at the hands of a Great War veteran who fought for our country at Iwo Jima as a teenager. At the time, people didn't have a clue about Post-traumatic stress disorder and his pain was witnessed by my mom. As a result, my mom developed a mission statement of what a family tree with her future husband might look like. My mom, a sixteen-year-old young lady, gave birth to the most beautiful little boy (me). She, along with her twenty-year-old husband, had a mission statement for their family—peace and prosperity for her children and her children's children. She prayed every day of her life for peace and prosperity for the next generation. This mission statement was her entire life's focus.

My mother's mission statement was woven on her heart and recorded on audio cassettes. Many of these cassettes can be found in the back of her closet with little white labels on the side stating, "Robin's prayer." She wouldn't ever tell you she had developed a mission statement, but if you listened to the tapes you would realize that she was on a mission. The mission defined (1) what she was doing and (2) who she was doing it for.

I've seen business-people roll their eyes when I talk about the mission statement. They believe it is something you put on a website or something to satisfy a marketing initiative. If the sole purpose is to fulfill an obligation, the leader shouldn't waste his minutes developing one. The mission statement must be authentic because the leader will be screaming it from the top of the ladder. A leader who 100 percent buys into the mission statement will expect his team to memorize it. When memorized, the team develops a filter aligned with the leader. This filter is necessary when making decisions for the company. When the collective group of people on the team believes in the mission, the battle for a successful business is mostly won before swords are drawn.

ACTION ITEM

Develop your company mission statement using the above process. Share it with your spouse or a close friend to confirm its authenticity. Print it and memorize it.

PRAYER

LORD, WE DO SO MUCH BUSY WORK. WHAT ARE WE

TRULY PURPOSED TO DO IN THIS BUSINESS?

3

VISION STATEMENT

---

*"Good business leaders create a vision, articulate
the vision, passionately own the vision, and
relentlessly drive it to completion." —Jack Welch[3]*

What is a vision statement? Whereas the mission statement declares who the company is, the vision statement is a picture of the future. The mission states, "We exist to. . . " and the vision finishes the sentence by saying, "therefore, we must . . ." **The vision statement is completely different than the mission statement.**

The vision statement may not ever be accomplished in the lifetime of the entrepreneur. It is an aspiration. It is not a self-serving statement of a revenue or market share goal. It is not built on a specific time frame like, "In five years, we will be . . ."

The vision statement must be unique to the company. If every other company can say it, then it is not a vision statement. For example, a bland, overused vision statement might be, "We strive to serve our customers and bring them an outstanding experience at the lowest price possible." Every business can say this vision statement.

Imagine if the company died and the community gathered around the casket to lower it in the ground. The officiant slowly walks to the podium. He shares a cute story about all the products the company sold. He might mention a fair payroll and a 401k. He might talk about low costs and good service. People yawn as they realize that the company didn't really live a life any differently than the next. Then the officiant pauses and clears his throat. His eyes focus on the audience as he explains the true vision of the company. He passionately expresses the love the company had for the community and supports this claim with an extraordinary amount of evidence validating that the company love was for real. The audience is inspired.

What is the purpose of the vision statement? It is to inspire the leader and the team to accomplish something bigger than what they could accomplish individually without a structured organization.

How does the entrepreneur build a vision statement? With an intentional five-step process.

Step 1: Choose a Sentence Starter

The business owner should begin the vision statement with one of two phrases: "Our vision is to . . ." or, "We will . . ." These can be changed later in Step 4 to personalize it.

"Our vision is to . . ."

Step 2: Identify Your Target Audience

Then, the entrepreneur must identify the primary target audience he serves. Unlike large corporations, he is usually not serving the world. He often serves a local community that makes up most of his business. A community is a group of people who share commonalities. Many times, they communicate with each other. They could be located in the same town or city, or they might be a part of an online community. All that matters is that they share some commonality. The entrepreneur fills a need in that community with his product or service.

> *"Our vision is for every person in our town..."*

Step 3: Ask, "Why?"

Why do people buy the company's products or services? The entrepreneur should keep asking, "Why?" until the answer connects to an important human value like safety, hope, peace, comfort, joy, etc.

For example, we know that an auto mechanic repairs broken cars, but why do people really need their transmission serviced and their oil changed? They need their car serviced so it doesn't stall at the traffic light. Why are customers concerned about the car stalling? Because it isn't safe. So what the mechanic does isn't turning wrenches and checking tires. He gets his hands dirty so his community can travel to work, home, and school safely.

> *"Our vision is for every person in our town to travel to work, home, and school safely."*

Step 4: Personalize It

The entrepreneur now has a skeleton of a vision statement, but it might not "feel right." He will need to personalize it. He can remove any words to make it authentic. He can wordsmith the vision statement to align with his company's culture. It is also worth bouncing it off of others. Some may not like it, and may want to change it. Feedback is good, but the most important thing about the vision statement is that it tugs at the heart of the leader. As long as the entrepreneur believes it, then it is good.

SAMPLE VISION STATEMENTS

"There will be a personal computer on everyone's desk running our software." — Microsoft[4]

"Guarantee the best flight possible for each and every passenger." —Southwest Airlines[5]

"... a world without Breast Cancer."
— Susan G. Komen for the Cure[6]

Step 5: Envision the Vision

This time, instead of picturing a funeral, picture a celebration. The company has succeeded in accomplishing the vision. What does it look like? My friend, Michael Sharrow, says that a vision statement will actually tell everyone "what it will look like when we get there." The leader, the team, and the customers will all be celebrating years of hard work. It will be at a banquet hall where everyone is enjoying a feast fit for a king. Someone stands up and offers a toast. Ding, ding ding, he taps a spoon on a wine glass. "I would like to make a toast! I would like to toast the entrepreneur and his team. On behalf of our community, I want to thank them for their effort through the years. I know it wasn't easy, but I know everyone appreciates the hard work they put into ensuring our vehicles were properly repaired. As a result, I want to celebrate the gift you gave us, the gift of safety for our families and our children." "Hear, hear!"

If the imagery of the celebration resonates with the entrepreneur, he should share the celebration story with the team. The vision will be an aspiration and may never happen, but it will ignite passion for the employees and the lives that are touched by the small business.

ACTION ITEM

Follow the five-step process to create your vision statement. Again, share it with a spouse or close friend. Memorize it. Print it on the same paper as the mission statement and keep it close to your desk to be seen daily.

PRAYER

LORD, GIVE ME A VISION OF THE "LAND OF MILK AND

HONEY" YOU HAVE CALLED ME TO LEAD PEOPLE TO.

4

WHY SET BUSINESS GOALS?

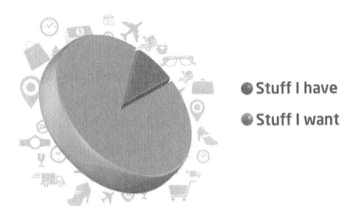

● Stuff I have
● Stuff I want

After the entrepreneur gets to the top of the ladder with his flashlight, he must develop a detailed plan of attack to escape from the foggy cornfield. This plan of attack is called goal setting. Goal setting is the process of identifying a goal and developing a strategy to reach it. Setting goals requires someone to make time to deliberately think out and write down how he is going to get where he wants to go. **Goal setting requires two important parts: (1) planning and (2) execution.**

The first goal I set was in fifth grade. Later in the school year, the teacher was running out of curriculum so we opted for a movie. Mrs. Fossler wheeled in the big box television and parked it in front of the chalkboard. The cutest little blonde-haired girl in the school, Rachel, moved her plastic chair right next to mine. This was fate. My enthusiasm was brewing. I couldn't think straight. The butterflies were gathering in my stomach. I couldn't believe she sat next to me! My goal was simple. The cold rain, the dark room, and *Where the Red Fern Grows* were a perfect combination to express my "like" for her.

The movie started at nine o'clock. My plan was to do what any man does to prove his boldness. At nine thirty, I would bravely put my arm around her chair, slightly touching her hair and possibly her shoulder. Nine thirty arrived. I hesitated. In my mind, I thought, "Let me first confirm she still wants to sit next to me. I will put my arm around her at ten o'clock." We could have been watching *Rambo* for all I knew. I wasn't paying attention; I was focused on the minute hand. Ten o'clock came fast. Unfortunately, I decided this also wasn't an ideal time. My arm might get tired if I reached it around her at the beginning of a long movie. Let me wait until ten thirty. Yes, this is a good idea. The minute hand turned and the clocked watched and laughed at my plan. Ten thirty passed, as did eleven.

I ran out of movie—mission failed. The tears in the eyes of my classmates told me I missed something special. Apparently the movie was really touching. I wouldn't know; I was a bit distracted in between the ears. I was disappointed that I never executed my good intentions. Yes, my first goal was never achieved. Rachel never knew I liked her.

I had set a goal. Setting a goal was honorable, and more than most boys could have claimed at that time. However, I got an F in execution.

I have since become better at goal setting. A little planning each year, compounded over and over again, made a personal impact that transitioned my life from a single-wide trailer in Castroville to running a successful company in San Antonio. I have never been in a goal-setting contest so I can't say I'm better at it than the next guy. I just do it. I don't forget. I consistently set goals.

There are two benefits of goal setting: (1) higher productivity and (2) increased confidence. Evidence supporting the idea of goal setting leading to higher productivity is validated by an experiment performed by Gerald Shore. In this study, three production groups were set up. Each group was responsible for executing a project and completing it within sixty minutes.

The first group was not given the choice of planning out the project. The second group was given the option of spending the first ten minutes planning. Before the third group started, they were forced to spend the first ten minutes coming up with a game plan. After measuring results and comparing the groups' productivity, the third group clearly outperformed the other two.

The second benefit of goal setting is the snowball of confidence that grows when a mission is accomplished. An entrepreneur who creates the habit of goal setting will experience the pride of looking back at the past five years on a job well done. He will experience the power of small wins in succession. Think about it. He gets to look back, see the goals that he set, and recognize that he accomplished them! This confidence is motivating and inspiring to the leader and his team.[7]

Goal setting takes time, but the investment of time yields better results and increased confidence for the organization. Once the entrepreneur experiences the increased productivity and team confidence of goal setting he will become addicted to making time to execute the goal-setting process every year.

ACTION ITEM

Schedule an hour and a half next week on your calendar. It needs to be away from the office and early in the morning. Label it "Goal Setting." Don't let someone take over that calendar time. It is a meeting with yourself.

PRAYER

LORD, MY MIND IS SO MESSY WITH CONCERNS AND

WORRIES. IN MY GOAL-SETTING TIME, WILL YOU

RENEW MY MIND? GIVE ME THE SOUND MIND NEEDED

TO FOCUS ON YOUR WILL IN MY LIFE.

5

GOAL SETTING: PREREQUISITE

Goal setting is distressing for me to write about. I am concerned the entrepreneur will do what I did for many years. He will set goals independently of God. He may potentially create a checklist of things to do to accomplish his own selfish ambition. Like I do all too often, he will discount the omnipresent Creator of the Universe who is interested in every decision the entrepreneur makes. Then, he will experience the disappointment of accomplishing things only the world praises. He will waste a portion of his life only focused on dollars and cents and not the lives around him. Looking back, he will regret the selfish season.

The good news is that God restores. He gives the entrepreneur another chapter in his life. This time, prior to setting selfish-ambition goals, he will change his approach. He will establish the two goal-setting prerequisites: (1) successful setup and (2) high expectations.

"Suppose one of you wants to build a tower. Won't you first sit down and estimate the cost to see if you have enough money to complete it?" —Luke 14:28 (NIV)

Prerequisite 1: Successful Setup

Distractions and a messy mind will destroy an entrepreneur's valuable time. He must take a moment to set up the right environment to truly experience the benefits of the goal-setting process.

TIME

A big chunk of time away from the office and distractions is needed. The business owner should not fill up the time only writing things down. He will spend much of the time just staring and thinking. It is in those moments that clarity comes. My goal-setting venue of choice is a hotel lobby with access to coffee. An entrepreneur's ideal place may be in a deer blind, a home office, or in his car. It just needs to be quiet and away from distractions.

PEOPLE

The entrepreneur needs to work with his spouse, his loved ones, or business partner to set goals. They will see things he can't. This is wise counsel. Did I say spouse? Don't discount the power of having your spouse engage in the process. I know it has personally saved my career.

PRAYER

The entrepreneur cannot disconnect the Maker of the entire Universe from his goal setting. This is a habit that must be broken. Prayer is the vehicle where we get to talk to our Heavenly Father about what is on our hearts, learn about His will for our lives, and see if the two are aligned.

Prerequisite 2: Set High Expectations

The entrepreneur may set low goals, discounting the greatness the Lord has in place for him. He has to think like a Texan: think big or go home. Pastor Tim Keller said, "I will no longer disrespect God by having low expectations (of what He can/will do)." The entrepreneur needs to be excited about the potential God has in his life. God wants to participate in his life and He wants the entrepreneur to live it abundantly.

We subtly recognize God when we say, "It happened for a reason." I'm suggesting that setting goals with God not be so subtle or reactive. We need to set goals that ensure the unique gifts God has given us are being recognized, used, and not wasted. Planning with God makes too much sense. Rather than simply meeting budget desires, the entrepreneur's goals will now include a legacy and others. With a goal-setting attitude in complete union with God, you are free to move to the next chapter!

ACTION ITEM

Invite your spouse or business partner to your goal-setting meeting.

PRAYER

LORD, YOU KNOW THE DIFFERENCE BETWEEN MY

GOALS AND YOUR GOALS. GIVE ME WISDOM TO

KNOW AS WELL.

6

GOAL SETTING: THE PROCESS

This idea of breaking down visions and missions into manageable and measurable goals was first developed by monks. They had a desire to be intentional about their fellowship with God and wanted to measure their commitment. In the twelfth century, they created something we use today—seconds and minutes. These tiny little goals were designed to accomplish a bigger vision—a relationship with God.

The entrepreneur will also develop manageable and measurable goals to accomplish his mission and vision. There are six steps to follow. The entrepreneur should start out with just a pencil and paper. He will clean up his chicken scratch in the end, but in the interim he will brainstorm. Brainstorming requires scribble and scrabble. He will jot down personal and professional goals as they enter his mind. The input will be messy, but the output will be organized and presentable. It will be something the entrepreneur will be proud of.

Step 1: Dream

The entrepreneur should start the process of setting goals by drawing a line down the middle of a piece of paper, creating two columns. At the top of the left column, he will write down the title,

"GOALS" (this is important). He will take about five minutes to write everything he wants to "be" in this column. The process may seem to take forever, but he needs to stretch his brain. The entrepreneur may want to be the market share leader in a region. He may want to have one of the best places to work. I heard of an organization that wanted to "be missed by their community if they ever left." That is a powerful goal.

Next, in the same left-hand column, the entrepreneur needs to take a few more minutes and write down everything he wants to "do." He may want to go on a vacation, put together a customer appreciation event, or move offices. He needs to write down his dreams like vacations, travel aspirations, and family getaways.

Finally, he needs to dream about everything he wants to "have" and write it down in that same left-hand column. He may want to have a new car, an emergency fund, or a personal assistant. The "haves" are personal or professional and could be endless.

"You gotta be before you can do, and you've gotta do before you can have." — Zig Ziglar[8]

Step 2: Establish a Timeline

Now, he will ask himself, "How long might it realistically be before my dreams can come true?" Next to each dream, he will write the number of years he believes it will take to reasonably accomplish it. To keep the exercise simple, he will use only one year, three years, or five years. Next to the dream, he will write a little number that represents how many years it will take to complete it. Ten-year dreams are nice but there are so many distractions that occur in life between now and year ten. The idea of trying to foresee life's unknowns becomes difficult. However, the entrepreneur has a hunch of what might happen five years, three years, or one year from now.

Step 3: Edit to Desire

In this step, the entrepreneur will open the door to his most powerful edit. He will draw a big fat line through the word GOAL at the top of the left-hand column. What he wrote down are "desires," but they are not goals. He will change the title of the left-hand column to "DESIRES," and title the right-hand column "GOALS." Dr. Randy Marshall, a corporate communication consultant, suggests a distinction between goals and desires.[9] A desire is not within our control. A goal is a set of specific action items that can be accomplished within our control that increases the probability a desire may occur.

For example, an entrepreneur may want to earn $5,000 per month in sales. How many calls does he need to make to increase the probability this will occur? The $5,000 per month in sales is a desire. Calling ten prospects per day is the goal.

Let me give you another love story as another example. Later in life, long after little miss *Where the Red Fern Grows*, I met another lady. The moment I saw her, I knew I was going to marry her. I was older and supposedly wiser. I had messed up a few dates in my day but I wasn't going to mess up this one. After a sweaty-palmed phone conversation, I convinced her I was somewhat normal and she agreed to have dinner with me.

I became focused. I cultivated a desire to win this girl over. Winning her over wasn't my goal, it was my desire. My goal was to commit to actions that might increase my chances of winning her over. My goal was to pick the best and most romantic restaurant I possibly could find. My goal was to iron the nicest clothes and apply the right amount of cologne. My goal was to have sweet melodies flowing through the car speakers and a polished interior for our country drive to The Grey Moss Inn restaurant. I had clearly established my goals. My goals were within my control, my desire was not. My desire was to spend the rest of my life with this girl. Thankfully, God desired the same thing. After a few more meals together and a private presentation of a ring, she said, "Yes."

Now that the entrepreneur knows the difference between a goal and desire, he must edit. For every desire listed in the left-hand column, he will need to list an associated goal in the right-hand column. There can be more than one goal for each desire but he must make sure that the goal is something within his control.

Step 4: Get Specific

After identifying his goals, he needs to get specific. Every goal must be SMACC-certified. To be SMACC-certified, each goal must be Specific, Measurable, Achievable, Compatible, and executed with Consistency. What does compatible mean? It means the entrepreneur can't write down that he wants to be a surgeon, raise a family of seven, run a restaurant business, and place in a triathlon, all while getting eight hours of sleep each night. Those things are not compatible for a man who hasn't walked on water. Consistency means the goals are accomplished daily, weekly, monthly, or annually. There are not random or "when I feel like it" goals. The entrepreneur must make sure every goal written down is SMACC-certified. If he can't SMACC it, he will need to revise the goal.

Step 5: Organize

The entrepreneur's piece of paper should be full of scratches and numbers and it should look a little messy. He will clean it up using Excel, Word, or another software program. The final outcome will show the desires on the left, the goals on the right, and somewhere stating the time frame for achievement. Because a small business is so closely aligned with the owner's personal life, there are many categories to consider. The entrepreneur could have weight loss goals or sales goals. He could have goals related to books he wants to read. He could have dates with his wife as a goal. The entrepreneur should include all areas of his life that he considers important.

POTENTIAL GOAL CATEGORIES

Spiritual

Intellectual

Physical

Professional

Financial

Family

Social

Recreational

Altruistic

Step 6: Display

Now the entrepreneur needs to type up the organized goals and "shower power" the list. He will go to Kinko's, laminate his work, and tape it to the shower wall. The evening shower will be the perfect sanctuary to always keep these goals and desires top of mind. His spouse will check out his dreams while washing her hair. This keeps the goals top of mind for her as well. The daily shower reminder of what is important to the small-business owner will energize his spouse.

The output is really fun to review year-to-year and see progress. The entrepreneur must create the habit. As he develops his goal-setting process, he needs to make sure that some part of it is aligned with his company vision and mission. This will bring everything together in perfect union.

ACTION ITEM

Complete the goal-setting project for one year, three years, and five years. Consider each category referenced above. Don't feel obligated to have a goal in each category.

PRAYER

LORD, DON'T LET ME GET SO BUSY ACCOMPLISHING

GOALS THAT I MISS OUT ON YOU OR OTHERS.

7

STAY ON COURSE: ACCOUNTABILITY

There is a region in the south of France that was known to be useless dry land prior to World War II. Today it is woodlands. It's a place where young families picnic under the shade of full, luscious trees. This wooded area started with a shepherd's dream. The shepherd was Elzeard Bouffier.

Bouffier would sling a sack of acorns over his shoulder and with a long spear in the other hand; he'd poke a hole in the earth. Then, he'd lay an acorn to rest in the soil. He made a point to do this consistently. He didn't do it for one month. He didn't do it for one year. Bouffier planted acorns for thirty years of his life. He did this all the way to 1945. Today, the oak trees stand twenty to twenty-five feet tall.

The oak trees grew into a forest. The forest brought life back to the streams by rechanneling the water. The water breathed life into a tract of land where children and family memories are the by-product of one man's consistent execution of a vision for a desolate land transformed.[10]

Bouffier had a vision of what his community could become. He realized that in its current condition the landscape could never reach its potential. He had a vision and was committed to seeing it executed.

Imagine the discipline that it took to see the vision through. He had goals and desires and he was able to stay focused so that he could achieve his vision. Few people have that focus and long-term discipline. Our company understands that we aren't all like Bouffier; we need accountability to stay on course. Because we often "chase rabbits," our team created two systems that help all of us stay focused on planting acorns in the ground daily.

Six Most

This tool helps someone focus on the most important things to accomplish daily. One of the most successful entrepreneurs in our country, Ron Carson, is the original chef of this simple recipe. This system helps someone focus on the six most important things needed to be done. Of course, there are more than a hundred tasks on a daily to-do list, but the six-most discipline keeps our minds and spirits focused on the six most important things to do that day.[11]

Every evening before we leave the office, we write down the six most important things needed to be accomplished the next day. Some of the items may be urgent, some may not. But by organizing the tasks before we shut down the computers for the day, we subconsciously put down our mental file of tomorrow's worries just a little bit. We don't bring the concern home of how tomorrow will unravel because we've taken a tiny but powerful bit of anxiety away from the next day and put it onto a piece of paper. Additionally, we've put a little thought into what needs be done tomorrow.

The next day, our morning coffee has a date with our six most important things list. All other distractions try to steal our time, but we stay focused on the six most important things. Our stress-releasing activities like paperwork or Internet browsing take a back seat to the goal-achieving activities listed on our six-most list. The simplicity of the system is beautiful. The key is the consistent execution and the accountability from leadership that the six most are getting done.

". . . and a wise man's heart will know the proper
time and procedure." — Ecclesiastes 8:5 (NIV)

Six-by-Six

This system is designed to improve the lives of our team members both personally and professionally. The idea came from Bill Hybels, senior pastor of Willow Creek Community Church in South Barrington, Illinois. Every six weeks, our team puts together the six individual desires we want to accomplish during the next six weeks.[12] These desires can be personal or professional. Usually, they are a combination of both.

Our team spins the Hybels approach just slightly. Our "six-by-sixes" can be simple. They can be silly. They can be fun. Or, they can be important and serious. They don't need to be SMACC-certified. Some of the six-by-sixes could be: take daughter on a date; clean closet; find a new office lease; or finish Excel project. The only rule is to do what you say you are going to do.

In our six-by-six system, we all hold each other accountable. We collectively announce our desires to the team. A healthy tension surfaces when someone doesn't do what they say they are going to do.

A leader of a company can set up accountability systems like the two referenced here or he can set up his own. Regardless, some accountability system is helpful to keep the team focused on the goals and desires it has set. The art of getting better has become lost in busy America. The key is for the leader to fully participate in the system consistently, with honesty and transparency. This authentic leadership will motivate others to accomplish their desires.

ACTION ITEM:

Start the habit of writing down the six most important tasks that need to get done tomorrow before the end of today.

PRAYER:

LORD, I LACK DISCIPLINE. I START GOOD IDEAS BUT

NEVER SEE THEM THROUGH LONG-TERM. GIVE ME

THE DISCIPLINE TO CREATE GOOD, HEALTHY HABITS

ALIGNED WITH YOUR WILL.

DEPENDENCE

"To this end I strenuously contend with
all the energy Christ so powerfully works
in me" — Colossians 1:29 NIV

The problem with defining the destination is that many times the entrepreneur never gets there. He may fail to accomplish the vision by missing his self-imposed deadline or by altogether blowing it. He gets the feeling he's only making crop circles with no end in sight.

The probability of coming up short is lowered if there is time invested in the planning process. However, even with the best plans, failure happens. The real problem is not so much the failure, but the entrepreneur's response to failure.

Every entrepreneur has had a brilliant idea and a foolproof strategy only to see the plan utterly fail. The entrepreneur thinks he has knowledge and experience. He sets reasonable goals, he does the right things, and then they don't pan out.

In 2011, we were losing clients to competitors who had fancy systems that could trade money more quickly. So, we hired a professional, invested in computer systems, and put together a program that could accommodate people looking for an alternative to traditional investing.

Our timing couldn't have been worse. Right when we implemented the program with a group of clients, the market experienced extreme volatility. It was going crazy as a result of fear of another 2008, European issues, and lack of political leadership. One day, the Dow plunged 520 points to 10,720—its ninth-worst point loss ever. A day earlier, it had soared 430 points. It was up and down like this all year long. We couldn't keep up.

Our strategy was not working. So, we decided to terminate it—but not without pain. Several customers were discouraged and we lost their trust in our competency. Even worse, the stress overwhelmed my business partner and he experienced physical ailments that required him to seek extreme medical attention. His colitis flared up and the inside of his large intestine looked like an eighty-year-old smoker's lung. While I shut down our vision, he was on disability for six months. Our well-thought-out goals failed. Our mission was jeopardized and in peril.

No entrepreneur wants to fail, but when he looks back at his life, he recognizes the greatest character-building moments were in those moments of failure. When our trading strategy utterly failed, we went back to our roots and decided that we were not going to try to play the market timing game. We were going to stay focused on the people and their long-term investment plans. We were not interested in the latest Wall Street fad of quick micro- wave-type investing anymore. Rather, we changed our strategy to invest like Crock Pots, slow and steady. No one will convince us to do otherwise.

More important than the business lesson we learned was that God got our attention. After we closed the failed strategy down, we spent time praying and speaking to other Christians who walk and talk with God daily. It was time to get rid of our selfish ambition and seek God's desire for our business. The conversations with God and His people gave us wisdom and strength in the troubling time.

Many times, failing is really God putting you on the surgical table. There is nothing pleasant about having your body opened up and getting picked at. The cuts are painful. But surgery is good. Surgery is often life-saving. God doesn't do spiritual work any differently than a doctor performs surgery. When you are on a destination of selfish ambition, God stops you, lays you down on the white crunchy paper bed, picks up the scalpel, and goes to work. He begins to pick at our selfish ambition and removes pride.

When you've been through a few operations, you begin to trust the surgeon. There is never enthusiasm in the process, but trust in the surgeon and his life-saving procedure makes the experience much easier. Failing is easier, because you know when the operation is complete, you come out of it more aligned with God's destination, not your own. God restores.

ACTION ITEM:

Read Proverbs 16:9. Study it. Think about it.
Memorize it.

PRAYER:

LORD, DON'T LET ME BE THE FOOL WHO DOESN'T

LEARN FROM FAILURE. DRAW ME CLOSE TO YOU

IN THOSE MOMENTS. I TRUST YOU.

PART 2: DOLLARS

8

DOLLARS ON THE BRAIN

The business owner autographs the front of the check for the rent payment and drops it in the mail. It's due tomorrow and it will be late again. He can handle the late notices as long as the fee is minimal. He's just relieved he had the money to pay his secretary and the rent. Next month will be a different story if he doesn't start generating cash fast. His customers owe him money but he doesn't know when they'll pay. He isn't sure how many invoices he sent out and how many have come in. This circumstance is compounded by the IRS. It's tax time and that money has already been spent to cover bills. Confusion invites his friend worry. The need for clarity is now. He needs help but he's too proud to ask for it. He keeps working. He'll sell his way out of the problem and will worry about money later. Why? It's just too complicated. It's too overwhelming. He has a vision and nothing will stop him . . . except the rent check that just bounced.

The complicated world of cash flow and finance overwhelms many small-business owners. They typically make their money by leaning on the right side of the brain. The benefit of right-brained businesspeople is they have a unique ability to be visionary, "big picture thinkers," and creative. However, it is painful for them to use the analytical left side of the brain that is required to organize and count the money. Like writing with the opposite hand, the technical side of finance is awkward and exhausting for right-brained entrepreneurs. Once the phrase "financial statement" is uttered by the accountant, the entrepreneur needs a G Force Gatorade and some Icy-Hot. As the accountant continues to ramble, the entrepreneur's brain begins to feel like he ran a marathon. He needs a temple massage with a cold rag on his forehead.

Just like needing to work out and eat right when we have to lose weight, there is no magic pill to get in financial shape. The process requires a little intellectual exercise of pull-ups and sit-ups on the left side of the brain. Consistent and diligent workouts lead to weight loss. Likewise, learning about money puts the entrepreneur in a better position to have more or, even better, to not lose what he has made.

Unfortunately, with today's lawsuits, global competition, and an IRS who keeps coming up with brilliant ways to make simple hard, ignoring the details with money is not an option. Entrepreneurs can get by for a while with "winging it," but those who do will eventually crawl out of bed on April 15 (tax day) with nothing but lint in their pockets.

We'll spend the next few chapters working out our financial brain muscle. We will jog a few laps around the financial statements. We'll sprint through numbers and ratios. Then, we'll cool down. We'll move our money talk down about eighteen inches into the heart. Once we're there, we'll learn about how generational change in our family happens when our debit card walks in moment by moment dependence upon God, because God is the one in control.

ACTION ITEM:

Get mentally prepared to work through the financial section of the book.

PRAYER:

LORD, GIVE ME DISCIPLINE TO, NOT ONLY WORK HARD,

BUT TO BE WISE WITH THE FINANCIAL RESOURCES

YOU HAVE ENTRUSTED ME WITH.

9

KNOWLEDGE IS POWER

"Suppose one of you wants to build a tower. Won't you first sit down and estimate the cost to see if you have enough money to complete it?" — Luke 14:28 NIV

The first part of training for our marathon starts with strengthening the great and powerful financial mind. By exercising the left side of our brains, we will build an understanding of the system of keeping track of financial transactions, also known as accounting. This understanding is the foundation that the entrepreneur needs to go the distance.

In my biased opinion, everyone should be taught accounting in all levels of school. Like the dressing in the Thanksgiving Day turkey, the knowledge in the school of accounting is stuffed inside nearly every profession. All of accounting can be summed up in three simple pieces of paper: **(1) the balance sheet, (2) the income statement, and (3) the cash flow statement.** The financial experts call them financial statements.

When a business-person understands the three financial statements and knows how to navigate through them, he outperforms or buys out his competition. He immediately brings value to any organization. There is a reason many chief executive officers (CEOs) were chief financial officers (CFOs) at one point in their professional careers. Knowledge of financial statements is a unique skill many other leaders aren't willing to learn.

In 2005, our mayor appointed me treasurer, and later chairman, of an economic redevelopment organization. Our job was to bring business to a part of town desperate for growth. Southside San Antonio is an area with a long Texas history, a proud family-centered community, but not enough economic activity to support the high-density and low average-income level. Our nonprofit became the landlord of about 1,200 acres of land located in this area.

The United States Air Force was the major tenant on the property. I had no idea what I was smoking when I said yes to be a member of the board. At our first meeting, I found myself sitting down in a room full of important people that I had only seen in the local paper. The board-room was organized in a U-shape. My seat was pre-assigned with a notebook in front of me containing the day's organized agenda, along with a multitude of supporting data. There was a podium up front and next to it an employee responsible for recording all of the day's conversation. The recording was important because it could be referenced in the future if there were any conflicts or misunderstandings.

This environment was overwhelming for me. What did I get myself into? My eyes drifted to a comfort zone—the financial statements in my notebook. The numbers began to come alive. I saw things others didn't. I realized that about 80 percent of our revenue was coming from the Department of Defense, meaning we were in trouble if they found a new P.O. Box. Not long after my appointment to the board, our biggest tenant did just that.

Fortunately, they gave us time and didn't pack up and leave overnight. We spent the next four years putting together a transitional financial plan. We cut costs by firing landscapers who mowed dirt. We built up a massive rainy-day fund. More importantly, we recruited other businesses to move to the area. The numbers drove our entire focus. Led by the CEO, Don Jakeway, our team successfully accomplished its mission. After the Air Force vacated the premises, the area could have become an asbestos-filled ghost town. Instead, it turned into a proud community with new job opportunities. Today, it is an area with traffic, a crowded Chick-fil-A playground, and like most suburbs, a Starbucks.

San Antonio Mayor, Julian Castro, named a park
The Darryl W. Lyons Park to recognize the work
done during this transitional time in our city.
I am thankful and enjoy taking my children to
slide on the slides and play on monkey bars while
I pick up soda cans to keep my park clean.

The good idea of redeveloping this part of the city worked because of the support of a sound financial game plan. This plan began with an examination of the three financial statements and a forecast of the future of those statements. The people who understand money and finance succeed in leading their organizations. Recognizing the power of knowledge should encourage the entrepreneur to navigate the three financial statements in more detail. This knowledge will kick his competition to the curb. It will get him past the IRS audit. The knowledge will help him weather a recession. He will lead his team, his company, and his family, simply by recognizing the value of knowing finance. Throughout the next three chapters, we will explore the three financial statements in more detail.

ACTION ITEM:

Quiz yourself. What are the three major financial statements?

_____

PRAYER:

LORD, YOU GAVE ME A SOUND MIND FOR A REASON.

GIVE ME THE MENTAL STRENGTH TO UNDERSTAND

THE WORLD OF NUMBERS, FINANCE, AND MATH.

10

THE BALANCE SHEET

As we continue training for our marathon, the balance sheet can be likened to the time recorded in the last race. It gives the entrepreneur a baseline for him to improve upon. The balance sheet tells others how much he has in the bank as a part of his assets and how much he has in liabilities. This particular financial statement also tells others how much the entrepreneur's business is worth in the event he wants to sell it. Now we will look at the three components of the balance sheet in more detail.

UGLY ROSES COMPANY		BALANCE SHEET DECEMBER 31, 2014		
Assets		**Liabilities**		
Current Assets		Current Liabilities		
Cash	$ 15,000	Accounts Payable	$	5,000
Accounts Receivable	$ 2,500	Taxes Payable	$	2,500
Total Current Assets	$ 17,500	**Total Current Liabilities**	$	7,500
Land and Building	$ 50,000	**Long-Term Debt**	$	25,000
Total Assets	$ 67,500	**Owner's Equity**	$	35,000

Assets

What an entrepreneur owns are called his assets. This includes cash, computers, and even something called goodwill. The Ugly Roses Company has cash in the bank as well as accounts receivable— money owed from products and services that have already been sold. In the case of the Ugly Roses Company, the total assets are $67,500.

Liabilities

What the entrepreneur owes are called liabilities. Liabilities are the same thing as debt, just a fancier word. The accounts payable is money owed to other people for products or services the entrepreneur already received. For example, he may have received inventory or supplies but he has yet to fully pay the company who sold them to him. Having excessive business-owner liabilities is like running a race with a backpack full of bricks. The entrepreneur will lose at best or have a breakdown at worst.

The entrepreneur with credit card and accounts payable debt works late nights and misses his children's school play. A plan of action, not of ignorance, is necessary. Debt won't just disappear on its own. The brick-backpacked entrepreneur must change behavioral patterns, spend less, sell assets, and sell products. The combination of these actions makes the plan come together. After consistent effort, he removes the bricks from the backpack and feels the freedom of running with greater ease.

In the case of the Ugly Roses Company, the total liabilities are $32,500. The balance sheet shows a difference between long-term debt of $25,000 and current liabilities of $7,500. Current liabilities are usually due within one year, whereas long-term debt can be paid out beyond that. Either way, all of it is debt.

"... the borrower is slave to the
lender." —Proverbs 22:7

Net Worth = Owner's Equity

It is not uncommon for people to confuse net and gross. The reason it is called "net" is because you have subtracted something to get to a specific number. Gross, on the other hand, is the top number in which everything else is subtracted from. In the case of net worth, liabilities have been subtracted from assets. Sometimes when I hear someone say, "He's worth a million dollars," I wonder if that is his net worth. If what the person is really referring to are his assets, then we must subtract his liabilities to get his actual net worth. When we do the math the right way, it is likely his net worth on the balance sheet is like everyone else's. **Owner's equity and net worth are the same thing.**

The Ugly Roses Company has owner's equity of $35,000. This amount is derived by taking the assets, $67,500, and subtracting the liabilities, $32,500.

Now that the entrepreneur knows the basic components of a balance sheet, let's walk through another example. My sister, Sarah, is an incredible up-and-coming entrepreneur photographer. In 2014, she was recognized as one of the most creative people in the city of San Antonio by *The San Antonio Current*. The reason I talk about my sister (other than to brag) is because her occupation best exemplifies how a balance sheet works.

Let's imagine that Sarah has inspired a young recent college graduate to start her own photography business. First, she needs to buy a camera. Being a professional, she dreams of a rock-star paparazzi-like camera, the kind of fancy camera where she could change all the lenses out and the picture gets so clear she can see in the future. She goes online and purchases a $2,500 camera with her debit card. This purchase gives her a little ambition and some boldness.

Confidence becomes renewed with the new business partner hanging around her neck. All the stomach butterflies are going and then, just when she gets them to flutter in the same direction, she realizes no one is knocking on the door. She needs to advertise. So, discounting the importance of being out of debt, she arrives at the bank right when they open and they lend her money on nothing more than her good word. She borrows $2,000. She takes the money and spends it on an inexpensive one-year ad in *Wedding Magazine*. What is her net worth? The $2,500 camera minus the $2,000 bank loan equals a net worth of $500.

Dated at the top, a balance sheet is a photograph (a snapshot) of the entrepreneur's financial life at a given point in time. The balance sheet provides valuable information if the entrepreneur desires to sell his business. Stephen Covey said in his classic book, *The 7 Habits of Highly Effective People,* "Begin with the end in mind." Even at the infancy stage of business, the entrepreneur needs to create a general idea of how to exit the business. Will he retire? Will he give the results of his blood, sweat, and tears to his children? Will he give the business to the employees? Or, will he sell it? Even if there is a remote possibility that it could be up for sale, he will want to know what his business is worth.

The entrepreneur's first-year balance sheet is his initial race time. As he compares next year's race time to last year's, he should see progress. His business decisions should drive up assets and drive down liabilities. The progress is inspiring as his net worth grows and he is able to see on paper the reward for his hard work, creativity, and risk of being an entrepreneur.

ACTION ITEM:

Create your own balance sheet. Quickbooks is a great tool. You can also use Excel software. If neither of these choices are comfortable, simply write down your company balance sheet on a piece of paper.

PRAYER:

LORD, DEBT WORRIES ME. I DON'T WANT TO WORRY

ANYMORE. GIVE ME PEACE IN THIS SEASON AND

STRENGTH TO RESOLVE ALL MY LIABILITIES.

11

THE INCOME STATEMENT

ROTTEN FRUIT COMPANY		INCOME STATEMENT FOR THE YEAR ENDING DECEMBER 31, 2014		
Revenues		**Expenses**		
Sales	5000	Auto Expense	$	1,000
Interest Income	$ 100	Insurance Expense	$	500
		Total Expenses	$	**1,500**
		Net Income	$	**3,600**
Total Revenues	**$ 5,100**			

The income statement is the second financial piece of paper that makes up an entrepreneur's accounting "books." The income statement has three parts: revenue, expenses, and net income. Like an ice-cold bottle of water, fitted running shoes, and comfortable clothing, all three parts play a role in the entrepreneur's race.

The first part of the income statement is the dollar value of all products sold totaled up to equal **revenue**. I may be kicked out of the financial industry for doing this, but I need to tell you a dirty little secret (picture me whispering). Sales and revenue basically mean the same thing. The second part of the income statement is **expenses**. These are all the bills paid. The third part is **net income.** Net income tells the business owner if he made money or lost money in any given year.

In the example of the Rotten Fruit Company, the revenue is $5,100 and the expenses are $1,500. After subtracting the two numbers, the small-business owner has a net income of $3,600 ($5,100-$1,500). One more whispered secret—profit and net income are basically the same thing too. Finance people like to talk with a lot of words. The more words they make up the more money they make. Finance doesn't need to be complicated.

A common desire for every successful entrepreneur is to drive up net income. There are only two ways to accomplish this goal. Sell more or spend less. The entrepreneur is already focused aggressively on sales, so he needs to recognize the power of consistent focus on the debit card transactions.

Spending restraint starts with a budget. It is irresponsible for an entrepreneur to run a business without a budget. But I get it—it's hard and overwhelming. Below, we will navigate through a sample budget. However, the challenge is that budgets are industry specific. For example, a restaurant will have more payroll than a law office. A doctor will have more insurance costs than a beautician. Therefore, the example shown is a starting point to strengthen our financial minds. There are many other resources available if the entrepreneur wants to compare his specific business to other similar businesses. A couple of those resources are ProfitCents.com and BizMiner.com.

SAMPLE BUDGET

Line 1	Revenue	$ 100,000	
Line 2	Payroll	$ 45,000	45%
Line 3	Rent	$ 5,000	5%
Line 4	Insurance	$ 5,000	5%
Line 5	Telephone & Technology	$ 5,000	5%
Line 6	Marketing	$ 5,000	5%
Line 7	Professional Services (CPA, Attorney)	$ 5,000	5%
Line 8	Supplies	$ 4,000	4%
Line 9	Emergency Fund	$ 1,000	1%
Line 10	Profit Before Income Taxes	$ 25,000	25%

Line 1: *Revenue*

The revenue number is key to making the budget work. Obviously, if the business doesn't make any money it can't spend any money. Therefore, every other item below line one will be expressed as a percentage of revenue. The revenue budget is created by reviewing last year's plan and increasing it by 20 percent. This should be a normal growth rate of a small business. I like to run my budget on three different scenarios: base-case = 100 percent of last year's revenue; best-case = 120 percent of last year's revenue; and worst-case = 80 percent of last year's revenue. Employee bonuses can be paid out on base-or-best-case scenarios.

Lines 2-4: *Bear Grylls Bills.*

Bear Grylls is the British adventure seeker in the show *Man vs. Wild.* The goal of the show is to educate the viewer about strategic survival techniques under certain conditions. In his British accent, Grylls explains to the viewer that the first and most important four action items before the brain dysfunctions are to find: shelter, food, water, and heat. The survival entrepreneur needs to identify his company's

Bear Grylls bills. These usually include payroll (food), rent (shelter), and other items to keep the doors open (water and heat).

Line 5-9: *Flexible Expenses.*

These items are the other expenses that could be eliminated or reduced if the company doesn't sell enough products or services. Most academics refer to these expenses as variable expenses and the other Bear Grylls bills as fixed expenses. Variable expenses fluctuate depending on the volume of revenue. For example, supplies or marketing expenditures might increase as business volume picks up. Also, I prefer to have an item called an emergency fund line item. This is a catch all item because inevitably not all expenses will be identified in the initial budget. Every year, there are always a few extra expenses that the entrepreneur can't anticipate.

Line 10: *Profit Before Income Taxes.*

Profit (net income) should be 15 percent of revenue. If it is not 15 percent, then the entrepreneur needs to go back and adjust expenses. In the above example, this small business is doing extremely well with a 25 percent profit. Again, sometimes different industries have different net income percentages. We'll look at this in more detail during our sprint through the ratio section.

The business owner can use Excel or Quickbooks to input the budget. Then, he must compare the budgeted expenses to actual expenses each quarter. If an entrepreneur can't commit to a quarterly review he must do it at least annually. One of my fellow entrepreneurs admitted to me that he had not paid payroll taxes for three years because he never reviewed his money. He now owes the IRS more than $100,000 in back taxes and penalties. There are many expenses that will sneakily creep onto the income statement that compounded over time, lower net income and put pressure on the company's sales, the company vision, and the entrepreneur.

ACTION ITEM:

Complete a company budget. Start out by summarizing the past several years of spending habits. Then, put together a spending plan for the following year and stick to it!

PRAYER:

LORD, GIVE ME THE DISCIPLINE AND MEMORY TO

STICK TO THE BUDGET. WHENEVER, I IDENTIFY

THINGS I WANT TO BUY THROUGHOUT THE YEAR

THAT ARE OUTSIDE OF THE BUDGET, REMIND ME OF

OUR PLAN. SOMETIMES, I FORGET.

12

THE CASH FLOW STATEMENT

"Business is all about solving people's problems at a profit." —Paul Marsden[13]

The cash flow statement is a detailed way to confirm if the business is making any money. Simply put, the cash flow statement tells the entrepreneur if he has enough money in the bank for the checks to clear. This financial piece of paper is one of my favorite charts a business owner can use to monitor the health of the business. The cash flow statement is the third statement accountants use to create the company books.

According to the Construction Industry Annual Financial Survey of 2007, half of the 400 contractors surveyed went bankrupt due to mismanaged cash flow. **Mismanaged cash flow is the heat stroke that shuts down an operation.**

A cash flow statement displays what money is deposited in an entrepreneur's bank account and where the money went when he wrote a check. The last item on the report is what cash is left in the bank after all the checks have cleared. The cash flow statement is different than the income statement, and the entrepreneur will find data on the income statement not on the cash flow state-ment. For example, if the rock-star entrepreneur who owns a music store sold a guitar in December 2012 but did not receive the actual money until January 2013, did he make a profit on the income statement in 2012? He may show revenue "earned" on the 2012 income statement but "cash received" appears on the cash flow statement in 2013. The answer ultimately depends on the guidance of his rock-star certified public accountant (CPA). However, the cash flow statement will tell him quite plainly, he didn't receive any money in the bank in 2012 for selling the guitar.

Startup International Dot Com Company	STATEMENT OF CASH FLOW FOR THE YEAR ENDING DECEMBER 31,2011		
	2009	2010	2011
1. Net Cash Provided by Operating Activities	$ 19,000	$ 24,000	$ 34,000
2. Net Cash Used in Investing Activities	($ 12,000)	($ 17,000)	($ 27,000)
3. Net Cash Used in Financing Activities	($ 18,000)	($ 9,000)	($ 2,000)
4. Increase (Decrease) in Cash	($ 11,000)	($ 2,000)	$ 5,000
5. Cash, Beginning of Year	$ 24,000	$ 13,000	$ 11,000
6. Cash, End of Year	$ 13,000	$ 11,000	$ 16,000

The cash flow statement acts as a high-performance heart rate monitor for the business. Both tools require attention to detail and frequent references. The above cash flow statement represents the kind of start-up company we often hear about on CNBC. It is like the technology companies where executives wear sandals, creativity is encouraged, and cash flow is erratic. Let's start from the bottom of the cash flow statement and work our way up.

In 2011, the company ended the year with $16,000 in its bank account. The line above this (line five) shows the amount of money it had in the bank at the beginning of the year, $11,000. Finally, line four shows that the company had an increase in cash of $5,000 in

2011. That is a good year compared to the prior two years where it had a hole in the cash flow bucket. Fortunately, the company had some cash reserves to handle that season. The company had planned on poor cash flow because it made large international investments hoping to get a return on its money in future years.

Burn Rate

Technology companies are good entrepreneurial case studies because of their erratic cash flow. One day, I was on the phone with the CEO of a Texas biotechnology company. He was pitching me to invest in his start-up. The company was selling a medical device used in bypass surgery. This owner was excited about his latest medical breakthrough and gave me his best sales pitch. I looked straight through his enthusiasm. I asked about the numbers. If the initial founder put in $5 million to start the company and they spent $500,000 per month on clinical trials, payroll, and marketing, how long would it take before they ran out of money? His answer was ten months. The $500,000 in this example is called burn rate. He hopes the Food and Drug Administration (FDA) approves his technology before the ten months run out so he can start selling their product. Without the FDA approval, he will need more investors or he will need to run to the bank and borrow some cash.

A small-business owner may not have a burn rate at $500,000 per month, but it is important that he understands how much cash his company is burning through each month. **Burn rate is a number he must know by heart.** He must memorize it and update it to reflect current operating needs. When he figures out his burn rate he will multiply it by six months and will have created an ideal **emergency reserve** for the business. He can call it a rainy-day fund. The entrepreneur may lose a contract, get sick, lose a key employee, and deal with litigation, all at the same time! Somehow, things like this happen together. Understanding how the cash flow statement works allows an entrepreneur to plan and prepare for future cash flow ups and downs.

Solving Cash Flow Problems

If cash flow starts hemorrhaging, an entrepreneur may find it difficult to identify a solution. He may become overwhelmed with all the information and default to "selling his way out of the problem." In other words, he will neglect other cash flow solutions and focus solely on selling more products to stop the cash flow bleeding. Sales will certainly help Band-Aid the issue, but tough leadership will keep the company alive. I love what author Charles Coonradt mentioned in his book *Game of Work*. He said there are five things causing business owners cash flow problems:

1. **Too much non-liquid assets (like inventory)**
2. **Receivables are not being collected fast enough (or a bad invoicing system in place)**
3. **Inability to raise prices**
4. **Unwilling to cut costs**
5. **Inappropriate management compensation**[14]

Every time I speak to a business owner with cash flow problems, I always go through this checklist. In most situations, the cash flow issue will be one of Coonradt's five. If we can narrow the problem down to the one major issue, we have isolated it and can get to work coming up with a solution. However, the checklist can only be used after an evaluation of the company's cash flow statement to ensure we accurately, not emotionally, address the problem.

ACTION ITEM:

Memorize your burn rate and evaluate Coonradt's five. Is there a gap in your cash flow you can tighten?

_____

PRAYER:

LORD, WHEN I STRUGGLE WITH MY CASH FLOW, GIVE

ME DISCIPLINE TO SPEND LESS AND BOLDNESS TO

CUT COSTS WHEN NECESSARY.

13

GOING DEEPER WITH RATIOS

After countless hours of training for the marathon, the entrepreneur needs a little reward. So he decides to satisfy his sweet tooth by baking brownies. In his brownie mix, the ingredients represent the financial numbers but the recipe is the equivalent to business ratios. The business owner might know his numbers, but ignoring ratios is like doubling the oil in the brownie mix. There might be the right ingredients but the chocolate brownies turn out really gooey (but I'll still eat them). However, they might not be edible if you double something else, like salt.

For example, the entrepreneur may decide to allocate $25,000 of business revenue for marketing, but if that amount is half of the company's cash flow he is mismanaging the firm's money. He might only realize the problem after he has trouble making payroll. Smart business owners will digest the ratio mixture long before they commit their money to a project. Every dollar needs to be evaluated relative to the whole recipe.

I had a friend in elementary school named Ryan. Ryan loved to tell tall tales. He reminded me of Chunk from the movie *The Goonies.* Both kids would tell stories about little green creatures taking over the town or Janet Jackson coming over for dinner. We started calling Ryan "Right Ryan." Every time he told us a myth the size of the Grand Canyon, we would follow up with a sarcastic, "Right, Ryan." However, we had an effective way to get to the truth. We would request evidence. He had to show us. Unfortunately, something always came up so he wasn't able to provide the evidence right then. But, "Don't worry, I'll have it tomorrow!" he'd say. "Right, Ryan."

Numbers have the ability to tell stories as well. How can the entrepreneur get the "truth" when the business world feels like a cutthroat, winner-take-all, master money manipulator? The answer is with ratios. For example, if Ryan were to say, "I have very little debt," he could prove it to us by showing us his debt and comparing it to his income. This helpful ratio is called the debt-to-income ratio. Ratios are always some number divided by another number. Ryan might show us his credit card bill and his paystub. We would divide his credit card bill of $100 per month by his paystub of $1,000 per month and recognize that his debt-to-income ratio is 10 percent.

When a business owner starts looking at numbers using ratios, he sees things totally differently. How do smart money managers, stock analysts, accountants, lenders, investors, bankers, and businesspeople get a leg up on the novice? They figure out ratios. An entrepreneur can become a healthier business person if he builds endurance by looking at ratios and interpreting their meaning.

There are hundreds, if not thousands, of types of ratios. Where does an entrepreneur even begin? Rather than suffering a heat stroke by evaluating the ratios available, we'll just check out a few. The two main ratios I want you to learn for your business are profit margin and return on equity (ROE). Remember, the main point is an appreciation of how ratios work so you can start looking at your money a little differently. Let's continue to push through the left-brain marathon and study the ratios.

ACTION ITEM:

Identify an industry advocacy group that has your industry-specific ratios.

PRAYER:

LORD, I DON'T WANT TO LIE TO MYSELF. REVEAL THE

TRUTH OF THE BUSINESS THROUGH RATIOS.

14

RATIO #1: PROFIT MARGINS

One useful ratio is called profit margin. **Profit margin is net income divided by revenue.** Profit margin whispers to the entrepreneur how much money he is making. Let's say an entrepreneur carpenter makes $100,000, but spends $85,000 on staff, materials, and overhead. What is his profit margin? The net income of $15,000, divided by revenue $100,000 equals a 15 percent profit margin. In this case, the carpenter keeps fifteen cents for every one dollar of sales.

Is this carpenter running a healthy business or does he have one business-foot in the grave? The answer is . . . it depends. **We should compare profit margins to (1) prior years and (2) to his industry peers.**

First, comparing to prior years gives the entrepreneur an awareness of trends. If the carpenter finds out his profit margins were 15 percent this year but were 30 percent last year, he can start doing his homework. Maybe the cost of his materials went up. Maybe he didn't charge enough money. If he is a student of the ratios, he knows how to fix the problems quickly before they get out of control. Like a dedicated runner, his training plan requires careful measuring and monitoring to not just avoid fatigue, but to win the business race.

Second, benchmarking gives the entrepreneur an awareness of competition. I run my business on a 25 percent profit margin. At one point, I found out about a competitor who was running his business at a much higher number. I was taken aback. I thought I had a good handle on our financial stuff! How was this possible? After a brief dive into financial statements and a few other details, the solution was simple: my competitor was focused on a different market in the same industry. He was focused on the uber-famous people who fly jets to his office; I was focused on those who drive ten-year-old Ford F-150s. In other words, our average client account was about twenty times smaller than his. We needed more accounts, and more staff and payroll to serve those accounts.

The comparison forced me to ask the question, "Should I be doing something differently?" I spent a few days examining my focus and direction. At the end of my self-reflection the answer was, "No. I am called to serve our specific marketplace." However, I realized that if I continued focusing on smaller profit margins per client, I must really be efficient in other areas to maintain profitability. I could do this. Our business model created a culture of frugality that would never have been recognized without a healthy benchmarking ratio exercise.

A carpenter should compare his profit margins to other carpenters, not dentists. Ideally, he would find it helpful to compare to other carpentry companies that are the same size as his. The financials of a sole proprietorship are completely different than those of a publicly traded company.

You should review profit margins, compare to prior years, and compare to peers. Many times industry advocacy groups have access to benchmarking information. You will just need to set a morning cup-of-coffee time aside to open up the industry studies and lay them side by side to your own financial information. The evaluation will help you make better financial decisions for your team, family, and future.

ACTION ITEM:

Identify the current profit margins of your business. Compare to prior years and other similar companies to identify trends and health.

PRAYER:

LORD, GIVE ME THE WISDOM TO BE A GOOD STEWARD

AND STRENGTH TO MAKE TOUGH DECISIONS TO KEEP

OUR PROFIT MARGINS HEALTHY LONG-TERM.

15

RATIO #2: RETURN ON EQUITY

Return on Equity is net income divided by net worth. ROE is another way to figure out how profitable a business is.

If a business is a cow, ROE is the milk . . . not the beef. Real estate people call this rental income. Commercial real estate investors call ROE cap rates. Stock investors call it dividends. Bankers call it yield. Again, finance people like different words for the same thing. Complication makes us feel smart.

A good business will yield 20 percent on equity. What is equity? Equity is the value of the business. An entrepreneur has several ways to value a business. One simple way to look at equity is by finding the item net worth on the balance sheet. Another way to look at equity is when the entrepreneur simply asks his gut. What would someone be willing to pay for the business today? Because he always thinks his baby is worth more than it actually is, he must reduce that amount by 25 percent.

Some businesses can be valued for more than just what is on the balance sheet. If an entrepreneur wants to get a little more technical he can follow accountant and author Greg Crabtree's suggestion. Crabtree believes the real value of a company is found by adding three year's worth of net income to the equity on the balance sheet.[15] It's a great formula and should be considered for those serious about tracking ROE.

Business ownership is similar to being a landlord. Imagine a business owner buys a cute little two-bedroom house in the suburbs for $100,000 cash. The home is pretty close to the university so he thinks he can get a few students to rent it without trashing it. He puts an ad on Craigslist.com and five minutes later, the home is rented. Now, he owns the home but he still needs to pay taxes, insurance, and repair broken pipes. Each month he collects rent, pays the bills, and pockets the rest. After he fixes the final roof leak at the end of the last semester, he realizes he made $9,600 in net income. The ROE is 9.6 percent ($9,600/$100,000).

The ROE sounds pretty good right? Maybe. What if the year is 1980 and putting the money into a bank account would yield a 12 percent return without the hassle of toilet repairs or a frat party?

If an entrepreneur's business only provides a ROE of 3 percent, he will need to be honest with himself. It's always a good idea to compare his ROE to other investments with the understanding of which ones take on extra risk and require more effort. What if he could sell his 3 percent business and park his money in a hassle-free 5 percent investment and get a job somewhere else? If he doesn't make the move, maybe he's betting only on the growth of the company. Regardless, the entrepreneur with a low-ROE business needs to start a robust conversation beginning with the question, "What is broken?"

Ratios can get complicated. Don't pressure yourself as though you must crack the financial Morse code of ratios to run a business or make decisions. Become a student of financial simplicity with a basic knowledge of the three financial statements and a few helpful ratios. Now, let's cool off and glance at money from another angle.

ACTION ITEM:

Identify your ROE. What is a Certificate of Deposit (CD) paying at a local bank? Is your return more or less than a CD? What can you do to increase your ROE?

PRAYER:

LORD, I HAVE INVESTED A LOT OF TIME AND MONEY

IN MY BUSINESS; GIVE ME AN AWARENESS OF HOW I

CAN MAKE IT MORE PROFITABLE.

16

BEHAVIOR > DOLLARS

"Broke is temporary and poor is eternal." — Robert Kiyosaki[16]

Now, the entrepreneur will start the cool down. He has spent the last several chapters building up the lactic acid in the left side of the brain by racing through numbers and ratios. The next several chapters will allow the left side to take a little break. However, this doesn't mean the entrepreneur is moving into a less important area regarding money. Quite the contrary. Money behavior is even more powerful than numbers. Personal money management expert, Dave Ramsey, says that only 20 percent of money is math and the rest, the 80 percent, is behavior.[17]

I'm a part of a generation whose collective decisions led each family to struggle with paying the light bill every month. Some of the decisions have been due to ignorance; some have been because of lack of opportunity. But in a country like America, the opportunities are boundless. I would suggest to you the financial struggles were mostly a by-product of behavior. My father's brother made a series of financial decisions that were a direct result of poor behavior and they impacted all of us.

"He's dead. Your uncle is dead, little Darryl!" I heard my aunt wail from her soul as she jogged toward me from identifying her husband's body. Despite being just a teenage kid, I was the one elected to be responsible for driving her to the police station. My uncle didn't have enough money. He didn't have the cash to make the deal work, but he still needed cocaine. In a desperate act of addiction, he believed he could snag the bag and make a run for it. He couldn't outrun the bullet.

I knew how Texas-tough my uncle was, and I would bet a lot of other people's money that he could overcome the gun. His toughness was known in our family. He literally grabbed a live Texas rattle snake with one hand while holding a Lone Star beer in the other. Despite his brief moments of crazy-uncle antics, I still couldn't believe he tried to pull off hustling a hustler.

Inanimate objects don't kill. Neither the bullet nor the cocaine killed my uncle. The money didn't kill. In the center of most awful tragedies, lies a story of man and money. This one wasn't any different. Money may not murder, but it can play a leading role in destroying a life, a marriage, and a family. It wasn't a failed escape from a bullet that killed my uncle, it was a chasing of desires to finance an addiction with abandon. Acknowledging the magnitude of money and what it can lead to, I take money very seriously.

My uncle was influenced by his peers. He made a series of decisions, encouraged by his friends that collectively became his behavior. My uncle chose to make those decisions, but I would suggest to you that he may have done otherwise if he had different buddies. I knew his friends. I knew they behaved the same way. As a result of their influence, he missed out on an abundant life.

My uncle wasn't just influenced. He was also an influencer. Unfortunately, he didn't have an opportunity to offer the kind of powerful and positive influence someone would want for the next generation. He missed out on the gift to influence his children and his children's children.

The entrepreneur can understand all the financial jargon in the world, but if he behaves irresponsibly his money will follow. In the next chapter, we will talk about the influencer and the influenced. The influencer of the entrepreneur's behavior is his social environment. Alternatively, the entrepreneur's behavior influences his family and the next generation.

ACTION ITEM:

Be honest with yourself. What habits are you financing? Could these monies be deployed in a better place? Are your peers influencing these habits?

_____

PRAYER:

LORD, I HAVE HABITS THAT I CAN'T BREAK FROM

WITHOUT YOU. I NEED YOU TO BREAK THESE FOR

ME. I KNOW YOU CAN. I BELIEVE IT.

17

> INFLUENCE

When a runner works out with someone faster than he is, he could be inspired by the healthy competition. Alternatively, when a runner works out with someone slower, he might easily get "pulled down" to the new running mate's performance level. In either case, like the runner, an entrepreneur is influenced by his peers in the race of business.

Negative Response to Peer Pressure

The dangerous adult peer pressure is subtle but it happens all the time. Counseling thousands of individuals about money, I am often asked the question, "How am I doing compared to other people like myself?" There isn't a way for people to know how someone else is doing because they don't get to look under the hood like I do. I study every dollar a family spends and every asset and liability on their balance sheet. I literally have looked at thousands of families' finances. I've worked with everyone from millionaires struggling to pay the mortgage to a couple who is madly in love and only living off of Social Security income. **The irony is that everyone overestimates other people's financial well-being and underestimates their own.** They end up buying things they don't need with money they don't have to impress people they don't even like.

Many entrepreneurs fall into the same trap. They see the neighbor with the pool and think their own kids will grow up wanting a tattoo on their face if they don't make the same "investment." They put a trip to Disney World on a credit card because they believe it will keep their daughters from marrying Justin Bieber's cousin. Many immature business decisions are made with this type of justification, and the root cause is a subtle peek at what the neighbor is doing on the other side of the fence. The collective result of these little decisions prevents entrepreneurs from giving, paying down debt, or saving for retirement and college. This negative response to handling money is unhealthy and too common in our culture.

"My problem lies in reconciling my gross habits with my net income." — Errol Flynn[18]

Positive Response to Peer Pressure

Because we moved around so much when I was growing up, I never had a chance to make memories with other goofy kids like myself. So I started my freshman year of college at St. Mary's University with a desire simply to be accepted.

Lucky for me, college friendships happened quickly and effortlessly. I am thankful for the friends I met in Daugherty Hall upper B (a.k.a. the Daugherty Minorities). It was amazing to hang out with kids who came from normal (if there is such a thing) families that had financially sound behaviors. Some of their moms and dads were doctors, business owners, and lawyers.

I had not spent an exorbitant amount of time with kids in this social sphere before I went to college. My feelings of insecurity motivated me to prove I was worthy in their community. I wanted to say "Yes," without hesitation if someone invited me out to eat. In order to feel accepted, I needed money. If I didn't have a little cash, I would be an outlier and a beggar to my newly found college buddies. I quickly learned about a bank right up the road from the university. The bank location was perfect because the distance was close enough that if my car broke down, I could jog there. A bank teller became my new brilliant idea!

Wanting to feel accepted reminded me of how previous generations felt "out of place." In fact, my grandmother used to stand out in her front yard with milk on her upper lip to ensure friends knew the milkman had shown up. This gesture was a subtle expression to prove she was worthy of being a part of the community.

Adult financial peer pressure creeps inside the family financial statement like a thief in night. Every decision becomes influenced. The entrepreneur considers his friends' position when deciding to send his own kids to private or public school, or whether to buy or lease a car. No one wants to deviate too far from the social norm. The benefit of enjoying life through hard work is honorable. However, the danger of keeping up through debt is dangerous. The entrepreneur must be aware of social influences on his wallet all the while maintaining a heart of contentment.

Influencing Others

Because he's an entrepreneur, his children are carefully taking mental notes of his training plan and execution. The entrepreneur must be careful that the adult peer pressure does not distract him from the little eyes watching him compete.

If the entrepreneur carved out a little bit of his brain and energy for his kids, it would have a ginormous influence on their decision-making process. This daily influence can get snowball momentum to change generations and leave a legacy. How much better is the legacy than a few extra sales? The wisest business-man in the history of the world said that a good person leaves an inheritance for their children's children. The entrepreneur may not leave an inheritance, but he can leave wisdom, direction, and leadership skills to his children and his children's children.

Unfortunately, most entrepreneurs do nothing. They think if they leave the kids a few bucks and a college degree then mission accomplished. But the facts remain, **only about 30 percent of family businesses survive into the second generation; 12 percent are still viable into the third generation; and only about 3 percent of all family businesses operate into the fourth generation or beyond.**[19] Wisdom gets stuck at the start-up.

Why does this happen? Because the entrepreneur considers hard work to be the sole purpose of his role in the family. He knows hard work is necessary to keep the lights on and the hustle drives him daily. While the kids are going to ballet and baseball practice the entre-parent extinguishes today's latest business fire. A busy life and a messy mind become the enemies of the entrepreneur's influence on the next generation. He simply runs out of day to teach the kids lessons. Unfortunately, when the entrepreneur is ready to teach, the children are all grown up and don't want to listen to the old man. So, the entrepreneur sighs, "Forget it. I'll just vacation, schedule a tee time, and enjoy the fruits of my labor."

Most entrepreneurs don't even have to teach about balance sheets and budgets. Rather, they can teach what they do know—how to communicate, how to lead, how to take risk, and how to work. Those character qualities are enough to spark change.

I believe the entrepreneur has a moral obligation to intentionally influence his children and family. The little devil on his shoulder will whisper, "Don't teach them about money, you are a hypocrite. You don't know anything. You make mistakes all the time." That whisper wants the people that the business owner loves to be ignorant with money, business, and make poor decisions so their families will suffer. The entrepreneur must not let the lies keep him from leading the ones he cares for.

One of the best ways to teach kids about money is through war stories. My father's war stories and battle scars inspire me to this day. His rejected key inspired my entire life. The entrepreneur must use his business war stories (good and bad) as often as possible to influence the next generation. War stories work better than a living room classroom discussion about balance sheets. War stories influence the next generation.

ACTION ITEM:

Start sharing business war stories. Be vulnerable with no expectation of response. The response is God's job.

PRAYER:

LORD, I CAN EASILY BE INFLUENCED BY MY NEIGHBOR.

GIVE ME CONTENTMENT ALONG WITH AMBITION. I

STRUGGLE TO BALANCE THE TWO.

DEPENDENCE

A business owner continues to worry about having too little or about losing what he has. The money obsession isn't even healthy worry; it's an anxiety driven, blood-pressure-cooker, bottle drinkin' kind of worry. Business owners can't pretend that a mind focused on the bottom line is "healthy." I own several businesses and to say I don't worry would be completely hypocritical. However, God has done some surgery on my worry gland.

I believe that my first step toward worry-free profitability was not something I initiated but rather was a response to God. After I graduated from college, my initial job landed me at a Fortune 100 company. I had all the success a young man could dream of as I hurdled the rungs on the business ladder. The plaques with my name on them included "rookie of the year" and other gold-star type of recognitions. People applauded me and told me how much potential I had. It felt good to be liked.

Despite my initial success, the memory of my father's experience haunted me. About five years into my career, I knew it was time to start my own business. I brilliantly (said sarcastically) dropped the six-figure salary. At the same time, my wife and I agreed she would quit her teaching career to stay at home with our firstborn son. Despite, my financial academic background, I ignored the math. With credit cards maxed and only a dribble of income, we just didn't have the cash to support our little family. We sold things. We gave away a beautiful golden retriever to a young family because we couldn't give the puppy the attention or healthcare it needed. We sold the BMW. We liquidated so much my infant child worried he would be put up for bid on eBay.

With a crying baby in the backseat, my ex-teacher wife would drop me off early at work and pick me up at sundown. Family carpooling can be awkward when you are in a business environment that expects you to cruise to the office in a detailed Lexus. I started my business facing immediate cash flow issues. Fear touched my face. I didn't have wealthy parents to bail me out. I sat at my mahogany desk on the fourth floor overlooking the city. I gently touched my Abraham Lincoln bobble-head. Despite his affirmation, the fear remained. As a man, I doubted I could provide. Worry took over and I became officially afraid. Random nighttime driving with the windows down pacified my fear. Melancholy Adam Duritz music on the stereo and street lamps became my drugs of choice. In my soul, I was failing as a husband and as a father.

I mentally quit. My wife didn't let me. We stood at the kitchen island around eight o'clock one night and I told her that we didn't have money for the mortgage. She listened to me admit my faults, my poor decisions, and my cry for help. Then, the Southern Belle spoke quietly but assertively. She talked of my dreams and my unique gifts. She gave me confidence and said that she believed in me. Her words were perfect. The confidence she had in me was sufficient enough for me to fall asleep that night and press on the next morning.

I recalled her words as I crawled out of bed. It was Tuesday, and I planned to refocus by arriving to the office at four-thirty in the morning. That morning, I took my wife's car. Unfortunately, her keys and my office keys weren't on the same ring. When I reached my office, I couldn't unlock the door. This feeling brought back childhood memories. Unlike my father, the problem didn't lie in a key not turning. . . I didn't even have the key. The key was sleeping at home on the kitchen counter.

I didn't want to drive back home in the darkness of the morning. I sat in the car and cried. Hours went by. "Lord?" I asked. "What now?" I didn't hear a voice from an angry old man in the sky. I recall Him comforting me as He spoke through my consciousness. I would call His communication an imprint. The imprint I remember was, "Put your money where your mouth is."

He hit me with a direct shot. I trusted God, but my wallet didn't. I said I had faith, but my behavior was inconsistent. I gave God my leftovers when the time and money was convenient, but never did I give when it required sacrifice.

That morning outside my office, I committed to giving first, systematically, and consistently to ministry work and those who are hungry. This commitment transformed my attitude about money. I know now God is in control of profits. I am not. It is peculiar how when I started giving to God first, my stress level dropped exponentially. I don't chalk the behavioral change up as psychobabble. I think God has the game of life rigged in a healthy way. I think He has rigged all parts of our lives to be dependent on Him.

My faith did not make me profitable. My faith, expressed in an act of giving, suppressed fear. **Trust is the antidote.**

"Anti" in the original Greek doesn't mean "against." It means "in replace of." We need to replace fear of profitability and money with something else. Because fear is a frequent guest in our house, we have to replace it with an alternative immediately when it walks through the door. We have to consistently trust God will work it out. Not random trust or "as needed" trust like a desperate passenger on a turbulent plane. But rather, moment by moment, trusting God to provide.

This act of dependence is a model for the business owner to experience money in a new way. It will overcome the pressure, worry, and messy mind so that God can transform his financial life and his family. The transformation is not a prosperity theology but rather the truth about peace and joy when our wallet is directly in line with God's will. Let's not let greed and fear blind us. Let's move to depend on God with our dollars and enjoy the financial journey of being an entrepreneur.

PART 3: DIALOGUE

18

SYSTEMATIZING DIALOGUE: THE INITIAL MOTIVATION

On a rare occasion, I had a chance to escape to the ocean. I was invited to go kayak fishing by a few of my semi-pro fishing friends. As regular visitors to TexasKayakFisherman.com, this crew had enough gear to open their own Bass Pro Shop, so I bummed one of the guy's extra kayaks. The small blue kayak was my traveling companion. Let's just say my wife would have called him "cute."

Our goal was to travel from a rocky shore in the bay to a little island about 250 yards away. You could clearly see the island as we loaded our gear into the kayaks. I figured I could swim across, but I elected not to test my manliness. Instead, I packed up my amateur rusty fishing tackle, my fishing pole, and my life jacket. I didn't know that the kayak had a hole for my stuff to be shoved in, so I put my tackle box on my lap. My fishing pole was in a little hole on the side of the kayak. Knowing that my commute was short, I elected to lay my life jacket on top of the tackle box on my lap.

The only obstacle we faced was paddling across a "cut." This is a deep body of water allowing ships and boats to shortcut across the bay. There weren't any traffic jams from the professional fishing boats so everyone made it through successfully—except me.

Initially, I was neck and neck with the group, but the faster kayaks started to separate from my princess kayak. I paddled faster and pushed more water with the ore, but I couldn't keep up.

Toward the end of the cut, about fifty yards from the island, a large fishing boat slowly moved past. It respected the civilians trying to enjoy a vacation, so it didn't run fast. But the mere weight of the boat pushed three-foot waves against my kayak.

It must have been the very last wave that hit me. It was just strong enough to flip my kayak. Quickly, I tipped over and was submerged. As I attempted to keep myself afloat, the tackle box hit my head and the tip of the fishing pole scraped my leg. My life jacket was underneath the kayak. The currents grabbed my ankles and pulled me further under water.

My heart pounded. Water started to fill my lungs and I tried to dog paddle through the current. In a brief moment, I was convinced it would throw me into the motor of an oncoming shrimp boat. Then, suddenly, I found a grip on the kayak. I pulled my head out of the water. Somehow, with my other hand, I grabbed my fishing pole, tackle box, and life vest. Just then, the waters suddenly calmed, the whirlpool subsided, and I was instantly safe.

A business owner can't have a team riding on separate kayaks. There is distance and noise preventing the communication and dialogue needed for the paddlers to arrive safely. Because of the wind volume and separation, someone might fall behind and get in serious trouble.

The strong and powerful entrepreneur may consider tying a rope to the kayaks to pull everyone along. Although communication might be slightly better, this strategy will exhaust the leader before the team ever gets close to the destination.

According to business succession planning expert David Grau Sr., JD, the solution is for the leader to ditch the kayaks, get everyone on a ship, and navigate the crew to the destination. In this approach, everyone is speaking regularly, working together, and arriving in unison. With less noise and distance between them, dialogue can happen more frequently and the work can get done with fewer errors. Everyone on the ship is contributing and plays a part in the navigation according to their own unique strengths.

Throughout the next several chapters, we'll look at how to find the right shipmates, lead them, and terminate the ones who are making the trip difficult for the company. The corporate world calls this hiring, leadership, and termination. You will find that many chapters are very high level and don't take you deep into the content. Your responsibility is to search other resources in the specific areas in which your business needs are most apparent. As we work through the following business concepts, keep in mind how creatively God has wired us to journey interdependently as we depend on Him.

ACTION ITEM:

Take inventory of your team. Ask yourself, would you hire this person again?

PRAYER:

LORD, I HAVE A HARD TIME COMMUNICATING WITH

THE PEOPLE ON MY TEAM. PART OF THE PROBLEM

IS THAT I GET IN YOUR WAY. AS I TRUST YOU, LET MY

TEAM SEE YOU IN ME.

19

> HIRING

Like it or not, most of the entrepreneur's waking breaths are at work. He's hanging out with people there. He laughs with them and at them. He breaks bread with them. He gets irritated with them, and they get frustrated with him. In a subtle way, the team members start to become a little like the entrepreneur—he rubs off on them. Motivational speaker Jim Rohn suggested that we are the average of the five people we spend the most time with.

When I was young, my mom realized who I spend my time with was important. As a result of her mommy intuition, she protected me from bringing down my average. I didn't understand it at the time, but today I do. She was extremely careful about the time I spent with my cousin. He was a few grade levels above me and he was cool. He was taller, had jet black hair, and muscles that tried to escape from his T-shirt. As children, we wore our Michael Jackson glitter glove and would fly off the roofs of buildings pretending to be The Fall Guy. When we were early teenagers, I caught him smoking. I warned him he could die if he smoked. In his best James Dean impression, he replied, "I could die crossing this street." To me, he was tough.

Eventually, my family moved and I lost contact with my cousin. Through the family grapevine, I learned he got in trouble. More trouble led to violence. He attempted to murder a teenager. The judge found no mercy and my cousin was convicted at a very young age. His head lay on a prison pillow for a decade. My mother's intuition was correct. She knew my average would be pulled down if my cousin was one of the five people I spent the most time with. My mother was the guardian of my average.

The small-business owner must be the guardian of his average. One of the greatest privileges of being a business owner is he gets to choose who he works with. The entrepreneur has a responsibility to make sure he enjoys the company of his shipmates because the journey is long and volatile. He must be careful putting together a team. He will be spending countless hours with these people. He must be intentional about bringing up his average.

"Leaders start by getting the right people on the bus, the wrong people off the bus, and the right people in the right seats." — Jim Collins[20]

Knowing the desired character traits needed in a good shipmate is the first step in building a team. I want people with the following attributes on my team: positive attitude, patterns of success, sharing of the same principles, and a track record of integrity.

Here are a few questions to help identify whether or not the potential hire has the character qualities needed to be helpful on the journey across the water.

SIPA Questions: Success, Integrity, Principles, and Attitude.

Patterns of *SUCCESS*: *What achievements are you most proud of?* The business owner is looking for a history of overcoming adversity. One person told me that he was most proud of being a championship video game player. I had mixed emotions about this answer. "Tell me more," I said. The response was uninspiring.

Track Record of *INTEGRITY*: *Are there certain types of people you don't get along with?* The entrepreneur wants to know if they will bad-mouth a former coworker or if they will speak professionally. He also wants an awareness of the candidate's own communication handicaps.

Sharing of the Same *PRINCIPLES*: *What books are you reading?* Why? First off, are they reading? If not, how are they growing personally and professionally? If they are reading, the books are an incredible insight into their character and if their character is aligned with the company culture.

Positive *ATTITUDE*: *Are you a lucky person? Why or why not?* Someone who says he is not lucky typically walks with a cloud over his head. However, a bright candle candidate might say, "I'm not lucky, I'm blessed." Or, "I'm fortunate." The explanation is where the business owner can digest the way the candidate responds to life and how he might respond to adversity under his roof.

Bonus Questions:

What do you like and what do you not like about your current job? The entrepreneur obviously doesn't want to assign them tasks that they dislike. This is a point-blank question to ensure no one is being set up for failure.

How much sleep do you get at night? If someone doesn't sleep much, he typically can't think. If he can't think then he makes mistakes. This question is more important than the business owner may consider.

On a scale from one to ten (ten being this is the ideal job and one being not interested) what is your current opinion of your fit for this job? If the top prospect replies "Eight," the follow-up question is, "What keeps you from being a ten?" Then, the owner knows how to focus the conversation to fill any gaps.

Education and skills for the job are important. I believe this goes without saying. The entrepreneur knows what the job is and understands what skills are necessary. However, often the owner of a small business can overlook cultural fit by focusing on skills and smarts alone. It doesn't matter how smart someone is, they need to buy into the culture. If someone's IQ is not anchored to a moral code of life, that person will consistently drift into gray areas of integrity. Integrity drifters don't fit into our culture. I have passed on individuals who were more competent or smarter than the other candidates because they didn't convince me they were the right players, or even worse, that their lives were not anchored to a moral code.

ACTION ITEM:

Develop a consistent interview process that protects your company culture. Make sure that you ask not only questions about skill, but that you also have specific questions to ensure they are a good cultural fit.

PRAYER:

LORD, THE RIGHT PERSON FOR OUR TEAM IS OUT

THERE RIGHT NOW. GIVE ME EYES TO SEE WHEN YOU

INTRODUCE THE NEW EMPLOYEE TO ME.

20

INDIVIDUAL PERSONALITIES

Before we bring someone on our team, we want to know if the candidate is a good fit. A personality profile is a useful tool to help reduce the huge, expensive mistake a leader makes when he "assumes" he has found someone special. Too often, the entrepreneur assumes that the candidate thinks and feels just like he does. Frustration occurs when the employee jumps on the boat and gets sea sick because his personality was misunderstood. Different personality tests are available that leaders can use objectively to understand how potential employees might think, feel, and behave in certain situations instead of assuming how they are wired.

The foundation of understanding one another begins with something called the DISC profile. This personality test is a behavior modeling system developed by psychologist Dr. William Moulton Marston, a Harvard graduate.[21] Every potential new hire, before they sign on the dotted line, must go to a website that asks them questions about how they deal with things in life. Then the computer system spits out a couple of pages and eerily describes exactly who they are. There are four personalities in the DISC profile. Everyone has a little of each, but some people have more of one particular personality than the others. There is no superiority of one personality over another.

Dominant (D)

The first personality in the profile is a dominant personality. These types of people are driven and no-nonsense Philadelphia Eagles fans. In the profile system, the Ds align themselves with the attributes of the assertiveness and power associated with a lion. Even though they mean well, they can come across as being cold. Oh yeah, don't tell them what to do—it will just tick them off.

When one of our new hires came on board, we reviewed her profile and she was a high D. I told her, "Look, I don't want you to go to Joseph (the president of the company) for things you might need for a little while." "Why?" she asked. I responded quietly, "Because he is a high D and you are a high D." She seemed confused. "Why is that a problem?" she probed further. Then I showed her a YouTube video of two lions tearing apart each other's manes. With a bit more explanation, she got it. I waited until Joseph and the new hire became more familiar with each other before I allowed them to start having robust conversations. Preventing the two Ds from communicating without a mediator in the beginning was a smart move.

Influencer (I)

The next personality in the profile is the I—the influencer. These are oftentimes salespeople. These people are social and have the curiosity of an otter. You can hear them ask questions like, "How was your weekend?" Interestingly enough, they are expecting and looking forward to an actual response. Someone with a lot of I in their profile can't wait to tell you about their weekend. In fact, they may tell you about last weekend and then invite you over to their house for dinner the next weekend. They are outgoing, but can be undisciplined. Sometimes you will find them standing at the door to your office just to hang out. Also, if the entrepreneur gives them a lot of facts, he will find the influencer, who can be easily distracted, looking at the squirrel out the window.

Steadiness (S)

Steadiness is the S in DISC. These people are thoughtful and patient. Their life's motto is, "Why can't everyone just get along?" They are loyal like a golden retriever, a reliable friend. Arguments, debates, and fighting are the arch enemies of Steady Eddie. Give them time to make a decision. Rushing causes anxiety and anxiety is the nemesis of a high S. Also, they can get analysis paralysis so please don't overload them with information. Give them bits and pieces at a time so they can think and meditate on the data.

Compliant (C)

The last letter of the DISC profile is given to those who are compliant. They are steadfast and meticulous like a beaver who thoughtfully builds a dam. They embrace structure and are comforted by organization. Don't give them inaccurate information or you will lose credibility. Also, don't be surprised if they leave early from the party. Often, these people are accountants, analysts, and technicians. Most shy people are always looking down at their shoe laces when in a conversation. But do you know how you can figure out if compliant people are extroverted? They are looking down at your shoe laces . . . ha!

The DISC profile makes the entrepreneur's job easier. It guides the leader, and reminds him how different everyone really is. To constantly remind himself and his team about these differences, the entrepreneur should consider displaying the profiles on the wall.

Like studying a work of art, when we get close to someone we sometimes experience their flaws and idiosyncrasies. However, the DISC profile reminds us that what we believe to be flaws are rather just the unique ways God designed us.

ACTION ITEM:

Complete the DISC profile for you and your team. Discuss the different outcomes. Remember, there is no right or wrong profile. Learning how to communicate is one of the greatest DISC profile outcomes.

PRAYER:

LORD, GIVE ME AN APPRECIATION FOR HOW YOU

UNIQUELY DESIGNED OTHERS. SOMETIMES I LACK

PATIENCE WITH CERTAIN PEOPLE. I CAN'T BE PATIENT

APART FROM YOU. PLEASE GIVE ME PATIENCE.

21

PROBATION

In the 1980 Olympics, the underrated US hockey team shocked the world by beating Russia. Hollywood recreated the journey in a 1990 film called *Miracle*. In the movie, Kurt Russell plays the coach, Herb Brooks. The camera shows Herb hanging out in an office overlooking the ice where the players are practicing. He's working with his assistant, Craig Patrick, as they pick and choose who makes the cut. Coach Brooks is done with his roster and Patrick is reviewing the list.

"This is the final roster? You're kidding me, right?" Patrick asks, clearly perturbed. Coach Brooks doesn't respond. "You're missing some of the best players!" Patrick exclaims in clear frustration. Without looking up, Coach Brooks tells his assistant with no hesitation or apology, "I'm not looking for the best players, Craig, I'm looking for the right ones."[22]

After the business owner has determined he has the right fit in a new hire, they shake hands and the employee gets to work. The owner is past the initial interview process and is investing more time and resources. Understand, however, the dating game is just getting started. He will need to set up the employee's phone and computer and complete new hire paperwork. The business could lose money here by investing in an employee who might not stay long-term. But the owner limits loss exposure by firmly establishing a ninety-day probationary period. Some of the better incentives discussed in the initial negotiations, like bonuses and retirement plan contributions, are not in effect during this time. The ninety-day probationary period is an extension of the interview.

The entrepreneur will be overseeing the new employee during this time and identifying how the person fits in the culture and interacts with coworkers. He will look for clues of concern like being late. He will monitor how the new employee handles pressure. The ultimate goal is to gradually come to a conclusion as to whether or not the employee has the skills necessary for the job and fits the company culture.

The entrepreneur needs to let the ninety-day time period play out because many people need that amount of time to loosen up. An employee who is getting comfortable can show his true colors. The owner may find that once an employee let's his guard down, there is less tension, and he is more effective. Alternatively, the employee can gradually become more abrasive because he "feels" the dating game is over. It is wise for the business owner to let this new employee reach his comfort zone; this zone becomes the tipping point where the owner can see if the employee has the character qualities needed for the organization's success.

The business owner will need to be actively involved in overseeing the new employee's duties. He will need to take the new hire to lunch, get feedback, and give feedback. He will take notes and passively micromanage. When you micromanage, picture playing curling. Sticking with the Olympic theme, curling is the sport where players slide a granite stone down a sheet of ice toward a target. They actively sweep the ice with brooms to move the stone instead of actually smacking it like a hockey puck. They consistently manipulate the direction of the stone toward the target. The entrepreneur will need to be an active curler in the ninety-day probationary period, moving the new hire toward the organization's target. By paying attention to the details, in the end, the entrepreneur will know if the prospect will become a permanent player.

Our company has all new hires complete three action items within the ninety-day period. First, they must read a book called *The Go-Getter* by Peter B. Kyne. Without giving away the story, the book exemplifies the type of effort we expect from people who join our team. Second, all new hires must attend *Financial Peace University,* so they can have a foundation for being wise with their money. Lastly, they must memorize our mission statement.

Having a system based on values and sticking to the process increases the probability the right people will join the team. Sometimes we make mistakes in our hiring; we do all the due diligence and we end up with a guy who can't go to the bathroom without help. We can lose people in the ninety-day probationary period. It happens. But God is good about having a hand in people's lives, even if the time is just a temporary moment at our company.

ACTION ITEM:

Set up a series of probationary period activities that align the new hire with your culture. If the new hire fails to meet deadlines, consider terminating the relationship.

PRAYER:

LORD, THANK YOU FOR BRINGING THIS NEW PERSON

TO THE TEAM. GIVE ME WISDOM TO KEEP HIM OR LET

HIM GO DURING THE PROBATIONARY PERIOD. I WILL

LISTEN TO YOU.

22

DIALOGUE: WHAT NOT TO SAY

"If you are not getting better you are getting worse." — Pat Riley[23]

As the leader of one employee or hundreds, the business owner is the influencer of the entire organization. The company culture is developed from the top down. In order for employees to break through their unrealized talent ceiling, the owner must first protect the environment so they can blossom. For example, how can we expect a child to learn if its parents are always fighting? If the child lives in a world of abuse and poverty, the focus is not self-mastery but rather survival. There are passive forms of abuse that permeate a company culture, and that abuse begins with gossip.

If the entrepreneur doesn't hear anything else he must hear this: protect the culture by implementing a zero-tolerance policy for gossip. This requires the leader to be authentic. If a leader is gossiping then his team will gossip. Even passive-aggressive gossip can open the window to other gossip.

For example, imagine an employee leaves the company and the terms in which he left disappointed the entrepreneur. He lost a lot of money and ultimately was hurt. In a passing conversation with another employee, the owner says something like, "Yeah, I would have fired him anyway." Would he say the same thing if that former employee was standing right next him? Let's be honest. If he would not have said the same thing, in the same exact wording, with the same exact tone, directly in front of the former employee, he gossiped. If the leader passive-aggressively gossips, he can expect this type of behavior to filter through the organization.

A business owner must create a positive culture by encouraging "reverse gossip." According to author and pastor Randy Frazee, negatives are handed up (to a supervisor) and positives are handed down and all around (to other employees). An employee might come up to you and reverse gossip about a coworker. This has happened to me. An employee came to me and said, "Alex is kicking butt. He is focused and knocking out his tasks. It would take three people to do his job!" That is awesome reverse gossip! I took this to the next level and praised the employee in front of everyone. I couldn't wait.

The business owner needs to set a high standard of integrity that brings to light even what might be "minor" integrity violations. These violations include, but are not limited to, lying, stealing, or cheating. An owner of a large company asked my advice about an employee who was issued an arrest warrant for stealing. The main owners of the company debated amongst themselves about what to do because the event occurred outside of work and they considered the arrest "none of their business." The lack of integrity was sanctioned. Do you think the other employees knew about this? You bet they did. The sanctioned behavior undermined the entire team, damaged good order and discipline, and threatened the trust of the organization. Just a few months later this employee was caught with a hand in the company's cookie jar—filling up personal vehicles with premium gas on the company's dime. At that point, the employee was terminated.

A team can't thrive if a high standard of integrity fostered by an intentionally built company culture is not actively reinforced by leaders of the company. The entrepreneur must stabilize the ship by protecting the culture from gossip and integrity violations so the team can enjoy the journey.

ACTION ITEM:

Announce a company standard of "no gossip." Not only announce it, adhere to it and enforce it. Then, announce a standard of "reverse gossip."

PRAYER:

LORD, I HAVE A HABIT OF TALKING ABOUT OTHER

PEOPLE. IN THE MOMENT, IT MAKES ME FEEL GOOD

BUT IT'S NOT RIGHT. GIVE ME WISDOM AND SELF-

CONTROL TO PREVENT ME FROM SLIPPING.

23

> HIGH/LOW

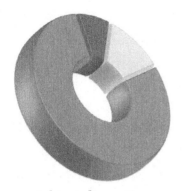

- Get-To-Do: Finish research report

- High: Customer sent me thank you note

- Low: Husband found spot on liver

Every night at dinnertime around the kitchen table, before our family of six grubs, we pray. Once we start eating, I never forget to ask my kids, "What was the best part and the worst part of your day?" Then begins the race to tell their adventure stories. "Me first! Me first!" Order is established by mom. The five-month-old just sits in the swing and observes the older kids as they battle to be first.

It's funny, because if I ask them that same question before dinner, their lips are sealed as they wait for kitchen table time.

The answers to this specific question give me an update on what's behind both the smiles and the frowns. The family dinnertime system provides me an opportunity as a father to praise the good but acknowledge and wrestle with the bad.

I also execute this same process with my team. Rather than questioning them around the kitchen table, I do it through email. Every Friday, I send the team my personal "high" of the week and my "low" of the week. Everyone responds back to me directly (usually the same day) sharing their own personal highs and lows. They can respond back using "reply all" for everyone to see or, if it is sensitive, they can just respond only to me.

The high/low system enables me to quickly get up to speed on my team's personal challenges. I am shocked when I uncover the struggles I would never have known about without this system. With my busy schedule, it might have been weeks or months before I would recognize things keeping them up at night, like children's behavioral issues, marital issues, or even cancer.

Next, I take time to individually acknowledge each team member's highs and lows. They need to know I am aware of their emotional state of mind. Most of the time, a simple email response like, "Bummer," or "I hope things work out," is all that's necessary. But, the degree of severity might require more engagement. If the high/low is meaningful, my response is more detailed. If it is serious, then a face-to-face conversation must happen.

Sample Email:

From Employee:

High: Closed large deal for company. Yes!

Low: Daughter was taken to emergency room because of a playground accident.

My Response:

Good job on the big deal! How is your daughter doing?

Unfortunately, business owners get too busy and we don't check the pulse of those around us. The high/low system provides us with an awareness of what is going on in the lives of our team. Deep-rooted problems exist that can only be seen when an employee opens the door and lets us in. People are human. Pain can't be dumped off at the front door and ignored on the job. Pain absolutely trickles to work. The entrepreneur must be aware of his employees' situations, care for them, and yet not let their problems inhibit their effectiveness.

ACTION ITEM:

Set up a high/low system. Give everyone on the team clear expectations of how it works. Let them know it is a tool to help you stay fully engaged in their lives.

PRAYER:

LORD, GIVE ME AN AWARENESS OF THE FEARS THAT

EXIST IN THE ORGANIZATION. I WANT TO SERVE THEM

WHEN THEY ARE SUFFERING.

24

CHIEF REMINDING OFFICER

My job is not to be a CEO, but a chief reminding officer (CRO). I remind my shipmates regularly of our principles, mission, vision, and values. All employees will ask themselves at one time or another, "Why am I doing this job? . . . It stinks." Throughout the year, there are three specific ways I remind the team of "why" our ship is traveling across the waters.

Advance

Our team doesn't retreat, we advance. So, we changed the name of our company retreat to an advance. We dock our ship away from the office cubicles and tackle strategies needed to execute the mission. An advance is a full day where we can discuss critical issues, but more importantly, readdress our mission and vision. I remind the team of my personal passion for our organization. I need to be red hot to get every employee lukewarm. The advance is usually held in November as we prepare to face new challenges in the coming year.

Kickoff

Fortunately or unfortunately, we don't have Christmas parties. Don't get me wrong, we love Christmas and we love Jesus. However, we have found people are extremely busy with their personal lives during the month of December, so we celebrate with a kick-off instead. This event happens every January or February when life somewhat normalizes. It allows us and our spouses to enjoy a high-class evening and dinner together. This event includes one brief presentation where I share my thankfulness to the spouses.

We also give out PAXie awards. These are clean, tactful, yet playful awards handed out to every employee. For example, Kevin was given the award for "loudest sneeze." Seriously, his sneeze shakes the building and yanks us out of our two o'clock weariness. Everyone laughed at the award as I handed him the certificate, shook his hand, and took a picture. Laughter is a required component of the kickoff. Again, I remind the team, this time with the spouses, of our mission and vision.

State of the Company

A few years ago, I informally surveyed every employee and the one thing they asked I get better at was my communication. They just felt in the dark. They didn't know where our company was going with all the little changes, disruptions, and new systems I came up with. I didn't know how to keep everyone informed without putting together another meeting. So, I decided to write a brain-dump email.

The "State of the Company" is an email I personally send out about one time per month. It communicates my vision and really cool action items pushing us toward the vision. The email bullet points the most salient updates on our organization and insight into crazy ideas running between my ears. Every person is addressed in the email. Below are a few real excerpts from a State of the Company email.

- Kevin is building the 401k business and working hard to create a system and process that ensures a good use of time. This model isn't extremely profitable but it serves Middle America — we have to continue.
- I appreciate the smile and energy that Janise brings to the office every day. It is contagious.
- We will be starting a rebranding process when we get clarity on the building. We want to coincide the two initiatives. I'm looking forward to the freshen up!

I had been jamming out State of the Company emails every month for two years when I began to wonder, "Is anyone reading this?" So I asked my team and found out that it was a highlight in their inbox. They loved the communication and looked forward to reading the comment connected to their name. "What will Darryl say about me?" Their encouragement kept me focused on the State of the Company email system.

The entrepreneur's workload makes it difficult for him to reflect on the vision and share it. The hard drive wipes out and an employee resignation distracts the entrepreneur. Every week, the entrepreneur gets caught up in the job and loses sight of why he wakes up on Monday and gets punished by Wednesday. If the leader is distracted, the team is drifting in the moonless ocean night. The advance, kickoff, and State of the Company email are awesome guides to shine light on the vision, not only for the benefit of the team, but also the leader.

ACTION ITEM:

Start sending State of the Company emails to your team. Make sure you reference every employee by name in the emails.

PRAYER:

LORD, AS I WRITE THE STATE OF THE COMPANY EMAILS,

GIVE ME THE RIGHT WORDS THAT ENCOURAGE MY

TEAM TO EXECUTE OUR MISSION AND VISION.

25

> TRAINING EMPLOYEES

"The Law of E.F. Hutton says 'Being in power is like being a lady. If you have to tell people you are, you aren't.'" — John Maxwell[24]

There is a difference between a boss and a leader. A boss yells at his new hire, "You messed up, fix it!" A leader identifies the problem and works with the employee to find a solution. A boss proclaims, "The reason is because I said so!" A leader provides a logical explanation and refrains from verbal abuse. A boss would never invest time and emotional energy into the lives of his people. A leader will.

When a problem springs up, sometimes the leader catches it quickly. Oftentimes, the seed grows into a massive redwood tree of a problem. If the leader is engaged, it can be caught quickly. If not, he'll have to spend a little more time coming up with solutions in order to chop down the tree. Regardless, big or small, all employee problems can be placed in one of three buckets:

1. **Lack of Skill?** The business owner may have a salesperson who is uncomfortable speaking in public.

2. **Lack of Knowledge?** The business owner may have an employee who isn't familiar with the technology that supports the business.

3. **Lack of Willingness?** This is a deal breaker. At this point, the employee has become impossible to coach or is unfortunately . . . lazy. The lack of willingness may have spawned an attitude of pessimism. Pessimism is contagious and should be quarantined, and if not resolved, removed from the premises.

After the entrepreneur has identified the problem, he can now help the employee hack down the tree with one of three saws:

Group Instruction & Drill (GID)

This is training in a group environment or classroom. For example, if an employee has a lack of skill in public speaking the owner can enroll him in a low-cost, well-organized curriculum like Toastmasters. Many times, industry groups will offer skills training. The key to the success of GID is having a system for the leader to measure progress regardless of whether it is through inside or outside help.

Individual Instruction & Drill (IID)

The business owner must set time aside for one-on-one training. If the employee is worth the investment of time, the entrepreneur must carve out a few hours from his own busy schedule, pay attention, and be patient. Many times, even though it feels hokey and awkward, the best use of the time is role playing. For example, let's say the entrepreneur noticed the employee is fumbling the product details when chatting with customers. The owner wouldn't want to just open up a product brochure and read to the employee, like a kindergarten teacher reading a story to the class, while the employee daydreams of a weekend lake trip. The owner would role play asking questions from a customer's perspective; the employee would bounce back answers. Role playing is much livelier, a little uncomfortable, but keeps the employee engaged so he can really improve.

Field Observation & Demonstration (FOD)

This solution is the most time intensive and really gets the owner's hands dirty. It requires the owner to take the day off of his current job duties and spend it with the employee. He will have to pull up a chair to the employee's cubicle. The owner will hang out with him as if they're in a three-legged race and study the employee's habits. Of course there will be a degree of awkwardness initially but the leader needs to loosen up a little, laugh, and make the day fun. With FOD, they will switch roles. The owner will do the employee's job and the student will observe the hot shot in action. The owner will make deposits in the employee's emotional bank account because down the road, as he continues to develop and train the employee, he may need to make a withdrawal.

One of Stephen Covey's seven habits is "sharpening the saw." The imagery is of two bearded men competing to hack down a massive redwood tree. The smaller of the two lumberjacks wins the competition because he took a moment in the middle of the race to sharpen his saw.[25] Some employees are burnt out trying to hack down trees with a dull saw. The employees need leadership to know their saws are dull. The leader must see what others can't, assist in the sharpening of the saw, and help employees win at their jobs.

ACTION ITEM:

Identify the deficiency of one of your employees and set up a time to resolve it using one of the above tools.

PRAYER:

LORD, WHICH ONE OF MY EMPLOYEES IS STRUGGLING?

GIVE ME AN AWARENESS TO UNDERSTAND AND

PATIENCE TO HELP.

26

TERMINATION

Acclaimed leadership expert, Dr. Henry Cloud, shares a story about a business being handed down to the next generation. The owner of the company witnesses from afar a man verbally abusing another employee. After a closer look, he realizes the abusive man is his own son, also employed with his company. The dad brings the son up to his office and says, "I wear two hats around here, son—the boss hat and the dad hat. I'm going to put on my boss hat. You're fired." The son stood with a dropped jaw, shocked. The father continued, "I will not allow employees to treat others that way. I will not allow you to ruin our culture. We tried to get you help, but it clearly isn't working." After an uncomfortable pause, the dad continued, "Now, I'm going to put on my father hat. Son, I heard you just got fired. I'm sorry to hear that. How I can help?" [26]

I hated the way my dad got fired. I'm certain the guy who made the decision was brushing his teeth at the time my dad's hand tried turning the key. The guy didn't give his actions any thought that morning because he didn't care. Well, now I own a business, and sometimes firing must happen. But unlike the spineless corporate midlevel manager who fired my dad (do you sense a little resentment?), I care.

As I write this, I am faced with the most uncomfortable part of being a leader—firing someone. An employee will be hurt. This person's family will need to find other ways to pay bills. Christmas may be challenging. I hate this part of the job, but I know when it is necessary for our organization. Three truths help me make the termination process easier. (1) I am a steward of the company and I must execute decisions in the organization's best interest. I only move forward after prayer and consultation with others. I take this very seriously. (2) I am not the employee's provider. God is. God will give him a job. I must trust Him. (3) I must be overly kind in giving financial accommodations to the terminated employee. As time passes, I would rather the person feel like an alumnus instead of someone who was fired.

Once the decision is made to terminate an employee, there is no turning back for me. It is time to move forward. My attitude changes and the burden of responsibility leaves my shoulders.

Several years ago, I had an employee who, if she were a cook, would have burnt the toast, blackened the bacon, and egg-shelled my scrambled eggs for breakfast. She made the same mistakes back-to-back-to-back. I had a lot of, "What the heck are you doing?" conversations with her. I even adjusted her role by taking a few things off her plate to better fit her talents. We Band-Aided the problem until I hired a few new employees as we were growing. The environment became the perfect storm for her. I knew she was incompetent but I never knew she was so aggressive. The other employees grabbed me by the ear and woke me up to the truth. The truth was she was not trustworthy, she was overly aggressive, and didn't even remotely get along with the other employees.

I personally liked to talk with her. She was loyal and seemed to always try; however, I had to make a change. So my sweaty palm grabbed the phone and I asked her to come visit me in my office. "Please close the door," I said, as I continued to look at my computer screen with nothing on it. "Look, it isn't working. We don't have much to talk about but I'm sure you know of the recent challenges. I want to give you a month's worth of pay and ask you to move on." She wasn't about to cry. Her eyes were stern. I thought I was about to turn to stone, but she silently stood up and walked out of the office.

Sure she was hurt. The transition wasn't easy, but I was confident I did the right thing for our organization. I was also confident I did the right thing for her.

I needed to be prepared for morale issues when she was terminated. I had to stay in close communication with the other employees. Some were really young and had yet to experience something like this. During the next week, my focus was keeping the team focused.

An entrepreneur needs to consider scheduling a company meeting to talk about the change. He must never say anything bad about the former coworker. Everyone will move on, but there will be a moment of pause by the people who look at the empty desk. The entrepreneur must maintain a spirit of optimism and keep hope alive. The end of the employee's job is the beginning of something new for the company, for the team, and for the former employee.

ACTION ITEM:

Before you are in the heat of the termination process, develop your company termination protocol.

PRAYER:

LORD, GIVE ME WISDOM TO DISCERN IF I SHOULD

LET THIS PERSON GO. I TRUST YOU WILL PROVIDE

FOR THE FAMILY.

27

DIALOGUE MEETS TECHNOLOGY

When traveling on a ship, sometimes it's difficult to have dialogue with someone at the stern when the entrepreneur is at the bow. Technology and systems can fix this problem, making dialogue between shipmates faster and clearer.

With only a limited number of hours in a day, I was struggling to find smart systems to improve communication with our employees. Then I remembered what a professional consultant and successful entrepreneur told me, "The system is the solution!" I'll never forget how the little old man reached out like he was grabbing a beach ball in front of me, emphatically selling me on the necessity of the system.

System: a group of related parts that move or work together. — Merriam-Webster[27]

Vendors, customers, and employees are the related parts of a system. How well the entrepreneur works with the different groups of people requires effort and creativity. He needs to be conscientious and systematic about keeping these important people top of mind. Systems allow the entrepreneur's mind to be organized so he doesn't freak out at all the junk thrown at him every day. If you look at the business owner's desk or office you will get a visual example of the current state of organization between his ears. Messy desk equals messy mind. Messy mind means that today he's distracted from the people God put in his life. Systems keep his desk and mind free from clutter.

A gigantic part (not a tiny part) of the communication process must be systematized. If there are challenging situations that are ***unpredictable,*** people can use their skill and judgment to react and achieve a positive outcome. However, if there is a ***predictable*** and recurring event, then the entrepreneur needs a system to support every phase. All communication, if predictable, must follow a written system and be adhered to consistently. For example, if the owner knows that every quarter he plans to talk to his top clients, he needs a system to consistently remind him.

The entrepreneur doesn't want just any system. He wants a system that works. He wants one that can be executed consistently and significantly reduces errors and miscommunication among the stakeholders. To a degree, he doesn't even want to think when he moves through the system so **his messy mind can focus on the other more strategic decisions.**

An example of a poor system is the sticky-note system. No offense to inventor Arthur Fry of 3M, but the entrepreneur just can't trust the Post-it-note-dependent employee. A sticky-note system is not a system he wants for the team. You've seen the person with sticky notes all over the desk, computer, and forehead. His system is designed to remind him and guide him. He "knows exactly" where everything is . . . yeah, right. You could call using the sticky notes a system, but eventually, it will fail with one orange note floating irresponsibly to the trash can by accident. Of course, that orange note will have a vital piece of client information on it.

Without a well-executed system, the entrepreneur spends much of his free time looking for things. Daily minutes spent trying to hunt down lost information add up. I get a little frustrated at myself when I try to find a lost email because I didn't move it into the right folder. However, when someone interrupts me and urgently requests vital information it is a relief when I know exactly where to uncover it. I then can get right back to my previous task without lost time and energy.

Technology

The entrepreneur must set up the system on paper at first and then use technology to do the heavy lifting. First, he will want to put some thought into the flow of communication. Then, he needs to hire the type of person (maybe a high C) that is excited to take ownership of implementing the system. Lastly, he will need to invest in the appropriate technology like Google Calendar (free), Outlook, or Salesforce. These are referred to as client relationship management (CRM) systems. The magic begins when the system and technology collide.

Great systems embrace technology as the backbone of the communication process. Technology minimizes the breakdown of communication and increases its effectiveness. It costs money to buy the technology horse, and the entrepreneur needs a jockey to ride it. Regardless, this is no longer a technology-free businesses world; if he wants to play today, he needs to pay. The business owner can't afford to wait and let the fear of voodoo cloud and application technology keep him from evolving. He must find the right innovative, useful technology and the right people to implement and manage it.

Let me give you an example of someone who failed to embrace innovation, Quian Long. In 1793, the Chinese emperor sent a letter to King George III that said, "I set no value on objects strange or ingenious, and have no use for your country's manufactures." This was a leadership decision that prevented an entire country from playing in the industrial revolution. Great big China lagged in the global economic expansion. China's apprehension of embracing innovation was a massive financial opportunity lost. Today, they are a leader, but not without having missed a century of prosperity enjoyed by the West.

The idea of setting up a system can be overwhelming, but if implemented with leadership and articulated to the team with confidence, the entrepreneur **will drive overhead costs** down and set the company apart from the competition. The key is for the entrepreneur to ride on the learning-curve wave knowing that on the other side is a wonderful experience where disorganization and mistakes are few and far between.

ACTION ITEM:

Write down all the predictable events that take place in the company. Then, create systems for everyone to follow when one of those predictable events occurs.

PRAYER:

LORD, YOUR PEOPLE IN THE OLD TESTAMENT HAD

MANY SYSTEMS TO WORSHIP YOU. YOU ARE THE

MASTER OF ALL SYSTEMS. GIVE ME KNOWLEDGE ON

HOW TO BUILD OUR COMPANY'S SYSTEMS.

DEPENDENCE

The first job I landed out of college awarded me with a hard life lesson. I was desperate for an old man (older than thirty) to take me under his wing, believe in me, and deliver perpetual wisdom. I read Michael Lewis' book, *Liars Poker*, and I knew, based on the book, if I didn't find someone who understood how to navigate the business jungle, I was going to get eaten. I found a hotshot, Louisiana guy named Tony with a smooth tongue and a slick suit. His suit was green and, to me, green suits looked cool. He said his suit was olive; I thought it looked green. After a few conversations and a couple of pancake breakfasts, he believed in me so much he hired me before I received my diploma. During this same time, my San Antonio Spurs had drafted a seven-foot-tall superstar named Tim Duncan. In an effort to show confidence, I told Tony I was the Tim Duncan of college graduates. This was nothing more than fear covered by arrogant rhetoric.

I chose the Fortune 100 Company after careful research and consideration of many other options, but more importantly, I chose him. I needed a hand on the ladder to reach down and pull me up. I had to figure out how to make a tongue silver, how to tie a tie, how to pitch a product, how to work, and how to walk. I was clay. I was moldable. I was amiable. If someone told me to jump, I'd be in the air before he could finish his request.

There were some tangible things I wanted in a career—a small salary, pay for my master's degree, and an uncapped income opportunity where I was paid for my effort and results. Tony confirmed that my requests were all a part of the package. Perfect—the promises matched my desires. I showed up on the first day sitting in the bullpen with another new recruit. This person was a few years older than I was and had just earned her master's degree. She, too, was attracted to the firm for the uncapped earning potential and guaranteed paycheck.

After two weeks of work, we both noticed our paychecks hadn't made it to the mailbox. We spoke with human resources (HR). HR had news for us. We didn't get a salary, we were straight commission. As a matter of fact, few of Tony's promises were true. We were disappointed, confused, and hurt. She quit. I stayed because I was desperate for a leader and role model. I forgave Tony and, in my ignorance, chalked it up to miscommunication. Afterward, I learned he had year-end recruiting goals that he met with aggressive hiring tactics. A few months later, he left our town because of ambition, more money, power, and another rung on the corporate ladder. I felt the footprint of his selfish ambition on my back.

Ambition tests the hearts of the best-intentioned business owners. As a result of getting distracted by the leather interior of the Lexus or the hum of a Harley Davidson, the business owner can find himself subtly overlooking the employees who depend on his leadership and love. Even honorable hustle can transform into selfish ambition that distracts the entrepreneur from the human side of business. The employees place trust in their leader with hope he will consistently honor his commitment. More importantly, they expect the entrepreneur to remember to care.

Confusion because of selfish ambition is nothing new to the human race. In the New Testament book of James, selfish ambition was a chronic issue. James must have been dealing with carpenters at the time. I can picture him talking to his team of fellow carpenters as they were getting a little wood from the local vendors. A couple of carpenters were ticked off at their product salespeople for getting them broken boards. Maybe product wasn't delivered on time. The salespeople were frustrated because the carpenters were always complaining. The carpenters were gossiping about the lumberjacks. The lumberjacks maintained perpetual jealousy over the carpenters' lifestyle in the city.

James catches on to the chaos. So, he sends out an email and gets all the callus-handed coworkers together in the conference room. A few carpenters show up, the woodworkers, lumberjacks, salespeople, and even a few priests (they were behaving the same way). Everyone stands with folded arms and red faces buried under thick beards. James calls for order. After a long dissertation explaining his observations, he gets to the point. The point is separated by a pause. His eyes show his seriousness. He makes it clear that their hearts are being choked by envy and selfish ambition.

We business owners can't simply suppress selfish ambition with our own will power. Ambition is tied into the character of who we are. Ambition is what drives us. To overcome ambition that gets coated with selfishness, we must walk with God moment by moment and pray that He loves our employees through us. We can't love employees like God can. Our role is nothing more, but nothing less, than a participating PVC pipe enjoying the flow of love. Eventually, our smooth tongue, olive-green suit, and business acumen will drive us to chase another business venture. Selfish ambition will stop up the pipes, but if we are hanging out with God, the clog gets flushed out quickly. As we become more dependent on Him to manage the people He brought into our little world, we see them not as pawns or tools, but as people with real needs and emotions. This **selflessness** comes as a gift when we move to moment by moment dependence on God.

PART 4: IDENTITY

28

WHY IDENTITY?

One Thursday evening, my wife and I attended a social function in support of a local ministry. The event took place in one of the most affluent neighborhoods in San Antonio. Executives, professional athletes, doctors, and attorneys were present. This event was held in a white 1950s home with large pillars in the front. The home was fully restored to balance the beauty between the original hardwood floors and the more modern recessed lighting. I felt like the Karate Kid when he showed up to the house of his rich girlfriend and nervously kicked a red brick out of the home's exterior. These formal social events are not in my comfort zone. It takes me a little while to warm up and get the tension out of my shoulders while networking with a group of successful people.

Nearly all conversations at social functions start with, "Hi, my name is (fill in the blank). It's nice to meet you. What do you do for a living?"

There isn't anything wrong with the intent of the question. It's our culture, and the question gets dialogue moving. Most people are well intentioned and just curious to know more. However, what if the initial dialogue started like this . . . ? "Hi, my name is (fill in the blank). It's nice to meet you. What do you believe in? What guides your decision-making process?"

Identity: the qualities, beliefs, etc., that
make a particular person or group different
from others. — Merriam Webster[28]

Okay, that is a deep way to start an initial dialogue but the questions get to the heart of someone's identity. Simply describing a business occupation (beautician, attorney, or mechanic) doesn't compel someone to become connected. It's the belief system that attracts and retains long-term raving fans. The identity is what makes a person and a company unique.

The entrepreneur's beliefs become the identity of the company. His identity is a result of his lifelong story. His dad's presence, or lack thereof, defines his confidence. The love of his mother shapes his kind nature. His experiences and the books he reads create the framework of what he believes to be true. He expresses his identity in his craft. People are either attracted to or repulsed by his identity.

Because an identity registers with others so powerfully, the entrepreneur must be aware of what makes him different. He needs to know his identity. Once an entrepreneur pulls together the principles that make up his identity, he gets the privilege of announcing it to a captive audience—his employees and his customers. As the entrepreneur articulates his identity, his company becomes an extension of those same qualities and beliefs.

In the next few chapters, I will share with you how to develop an identity as a leader. Then, the leader must build an identity as a team. The team's identity must be an extension of the leader's so there will be consistent decision making. Next, we will discuss how to develop an identity as a company. Lastly, we have to put the identity in place so it doesn't become cute little sayings at the end of an email. The final few chapters will discuss the attack on the collective identity of small business and what we can do to fight the battle as fellow entrepreneurs.

ACTION ITEM:

Think about your life experiences and how they shaped your belief system.

PRAYER:

LORD, I DON'T KNOW IF MY BELIEF SYSTEM IS ALIGNED

WITH YOURS. REVEAL TO ME YOUR TRUTH THROUGH

OTHER PEOPLE AND YOUR WORD.

29

> LEADERSHIP IDENTITY

"For we are God's handiwork, created in Christ Jesus to do good works, which God prepared in advance for us to do." — Ephesians 2:10 NIV

When I turn on the TV to watch the talking suits, I have come to believe more and more the truth that everything rises and falls with leadership. Everything includes families, communities, and business. That is a lot of responsibility to put on the shoulders of one person. But how that person responds to the responsibility is what makes him a leader.

One of my favorite leadership frameworks came from Larry Bossidy, the former CEO of Honeywell. He said the four character qualities that make up emotional fortitude are self-awareness, authenticity, self-mastery, and humility.[29] I think of these qualities slightly differently. I think of them as an audit of a leader's identity in Christ. Let's look at each of these qualities in more detail.

Self-awareness

Self-awareness is challenging for a leader. He gets subliminal messages from Hollywood and TV on who he should be or how he should act. If he doesn't have self-awareness, he will wake up one morning not knowing if it will be a J.R. Ewing day or a Donald Trump day. Early in my career, I watched a Wall Street movie called *Boiler Room*, and I found myself saying these immature quotes around the office like, "Lunch is for wimps!" or "What do you mean, you're gonna pass? Alan, the only people making money passing are NFL quarterbacks and I don't see a number on your back!" Those were the PG versions of the quotes. I was influenced by a movie at twenty-two years old. It's subtle, but without self-awareness, the entrepreneur will behave differently depending on the last movie he watched, the environment, circumstances, and the people around him.

Self-awareness for the entrepreneur is the process of identifying who he is. God knows what talents the entrepreneur was given and He desires for the entrepreneur to know those talents as well. When the small-business owner figures it out, God gets excited. When his unique talents are buried, the entrepreneur absolutely cannot experience the fullness of life that God has in store for him. The entrepreneur who embraces God's unique design gets a smile from God. It brings God glory. How does a tree glorify God? By being a tree. How does a leader glorify God? By being the leader God intended him to be.

Self-awareness gives the leader a better understanding of his true identity. He embraces his talents. He doesn't feel worthless when someone rejects him. He is aware of how God made him and he likes it.

Authenticity

Authenticity is an extension of self-awareness. However, instead of just recognizing the talents and gifts given to the entrepreneur by God, he is living out those talents, not trying to be someone else.

A good example of someone who embraced his authenticity is my brother, Franklin. Franklin is an artist. He knew he was an artist even as a child, and he nurtured his talent by learning how to draw, paint, sculpt, and design. One of the paintings he created in college can be found in my office lobby today. It is a beautiful painting of Abraham Lincoln on a shiny penny that clearly states, "In God We Trust."

Franklin stayed true to his innate gifts as he became a man. Still an artist, still authentic, but knowing that starving artists have skinny children, he diligently researched where modern art was progressing. This authentic research led him to an entrepreneurial career that deals with the merging of art and technology. Although his career path changed, he never deviated from who he was. His authenticity is impressive and he doesn't claim to be someone else. He didn't become a corporate finance guy. He didn't desire to become a banker. He knew who he was and decided that he would authentically live that out.

I believe when we get to heaven, God isn't going to ask why you weren't more like Mother Teresa. He is going to ask why you weren't more like you.

I love being authentic. Am I all the time? No. There are clearly things I am not good at. But when I try to fake it and pretend to be someone I'm not, I always get exposed. It is embarrassing when this happens. Alternatively, I feel a breath of fresh air when

I am authentic and share with others the things I'm not excellent at (like golf) so I can focus on the gifts God has given me.

Self-mastery

The third attribute, self-mastery, is a fancy way of saying, "I'm getting better every day." My brother made a point to figure out how to follow his dream. He had self-awareness—he was an artist. He was authentic—he wasn't ashamed of who he was. He recognized, however, traditional education couldn't support the way he wanted to develop skills and maximize his ability. So, he read, studied, and learned on his own. He stayed up late, and read some more. He realized the graphic design business was moving in another direction—mobile applications and virtual augmented reality. Without a wingman, a corporate training department, or a collective network of rich family members, he ventured into the development world on his own.

His pursuit of self-mastery paid off. A Fortune 100 company has flown him around the world to consult with its development team. He works in rooms full of engineers and PhDs from the Mid West to the Far East. He also developed several successful applications for use on mobile devices along with ancillary mobile application technology that has been featured by Amazon and other reputable third parties. He's recently started a new company that may change the face of wearable computing. In his ongoing pursuit of self-mastery, he continues on a path of success.

Self-mastery requires the pursuit of knowledge and wisdom. The pursuit of knowledge says that the entrepreneur is only as good as he is today **except for the books he reads and the people he meets.** The pursuit of wisdom says that the **fear of the Lord** is the beginning of wisdom. As leaders grow in knowledge and wisdom they will become more and more aligned with the unique identity God gave them.

Humility

The fall of many successful people is a lack of humility sandwiched between two slices of pride. My mentor ate this sandwich. He had it all—a house in a gated community, a beautiful brunette wife, kids in student council, a shiny BMW convertible, good looks, and a silver tongue. I looked up to him. I told him eye-to-eye, man-to-man, I wanted to be like him. But somehow the altitude of his success affected his senses. He fell. He fell hard. An affair with his secretary and ego-driven behavior patterns led to his own personal bottomless pit. His resume now includes a divorce, bankruptcy, and embarrassment.

My mentor taught me a lesson I will never forget. All God desired was for him to say, "It's not about me Lord. It's about you." Acknowledging who is in control is humility. When you are that successful the only way to stay alive is through humility. The irony is that the Latin word for humility is—humus. Humus also describes the decayed leaves and vegetable matter feeding roots and plants. So, just as humus is vital to the health of a vegetable, humility is vital to the health of a small-business owner's identity.[30]

ACTION ITEM:

Identify which of the four leader qualities you struggle with right now. Share this to your spouse or loved one and find out if that person agrees with you.

PRAYER:

LORD, I STRUGGLE TO IDENTIFY MY TALENTS. SHOW

ME THE UNIQUE CHARACTER QUALITIES YOU HAVE

GIVEN ME AS A LEADER. I DON'T WANT TO BURY MY

GIFTS.

30

TEAM IDENTITY

A team identity can be put together by developing anchors for the ship. Strategic anchors, defined by business management author, Patrick Lencioni, are the lenses and filters with which all decisions are made.[31]

At our last advance, our team gathered together around several round tables bright and early in the morning. The stage was set and everyone had pens, papers, and diet sodas within grabbing distance. I stood up in front of the team next to a bunch of flip charts. With a blue marker in hand I wrote down a list of potential strategic anchors. I kicked off the brainstorming; the team picked up steam and threw out more ideas. We debated on which anchors would be most beneficial to our organization. Because the team was engaged in the process, they were in fact creating their own identity. This process lasted several hours. We eliminated some anchors and eventually came up with a final list: (1) prayer (2) frugality and (3) community.

SAMPLE STRATEGIC ANCHOR
DECISION-MAKING PROCESS

Decision: *We are seeking to fill a vacant job position.*

ANCHORS

PRAYER: *Lord, please bring the person here who fits our culture and needs a job.*

FRUGALITY: *The entrepreneur would examine what similar jobs are paying in his industry, set a budget, and stick to it.*

COMMUNITY: *The entrepreneur would go to his church, his gym, and his neighborhood letting people know that the company is hiring.*

The anchors give focus to an entrepreneur's activities. Then, the team will also lean on the anchors as a part of their identity because they were fully engaged in developing them.

If a buying decision is in direct conflict with one of the strategic anchors, the team passes. If a new project would violate an anchor, the team passes on that as well. This exercise is more than a feel-good experience. Strategic anchors are the key part of the team identity.

Some might say if you just do the right thing, everything works out. Unfortunately, organizations evolve and people drift. Small-business owners need anchors to keep them from floating away from the value system their moms and grandmas taught them.

ACTION ITEM:

Read Patrick Lencioni's book, *The Advantage* **and work with your team to develop a list of strategic anchors.**

PRAYER:

LORD, PLEASE ALIGN ALL THE PEOPLE ON OUR TEAM

TO A COMMON SET OF VALUES. MY DESIRE IS FOR US

TO WORK FOR YOU IN UNISON.

31

COMPANY IDENTITY

In a water cooler conversation with one of my employees, I asked about the difference between the culture at our office and his former employer's office culture. I wasn't looking for a pat on the back; I wanted to understand specifically why he left and came to work with us.

He began to explain, "They started out having family picnics and flexible work hours but in time, they changed." He paused before continuing. "They demanded I stay late on a regular basis. I didn't mind at first. I was happy to help, however, I eventually had to start working weekends. I missed my family but, like a good employee, I did what I needed to do for the team. This continued for months, until one day my wife received a dreaded phone call. It was the company on the other end. They told her that I was being sent to the emergency room in an ambulance. They said I had had a heart attack.

"Sure, I'm a bit overweight," he said, as he put his hands on his belly. "But I'm under forty and I'm not supposed to have a heart attack at my age. The doctor delivered the results of my evaluation as I held my wife's hand in mine. A heart attack was ruled out and overwork, lack of sleep, and stress were ruled in. I had to leave the company. My family and my life needed change."

How does a family-friendly business evolve into a damaging, life-threatening culture? When the leader never establishes a firm and authentic set of company principles to guide their decision-making process. As a result of being blinded by profits, their ship drifts to a deserted island with palm trees of chaos and irritable inhabitants.

Mark Twain filed for bankruptcy and inquiring minds asked him how it happened. He replied, **"Slowly but all of a sudden."** The same can occur with a company identity if it's not protected. The identity is caring and loving, then, slowly, but all of a sudden, it can turn toxic.

But, there is hope for small business. It is possible to maintain the same value system it was founded upon. I believe the Bible is the ultimate playbook for how to run an organization. The middle of the Bible opens to the book of Psalms. There is poetry from King David in it, but the next book, Proverbs, is pure wisdom. Proverbs is full of principles for any business owner, atheist, or believer.

Rather than walking the halls, opening up the Bible, and pounding it on everyone's forehead, our company decided to create our internal mini-playbook. In the early stages of our business our company didn't have an HR department or even an employee manual. We knew we needed something that told everyone what the rules were in the office. So we put together forty-one of our most important principles. These were simply things we believed to be true. They became the starting point for our company identity.

Some of the principles are theological points like, "If you don't surrender to Christ, you surrender to chaos." Others are simple phrases like, "Finish strong." These principles are not just little cute sayings. They have become the foundation of how we make decisions as a company.

Another one of our principles is, "Robust conversation surfaces reality." When a couple of employees argue, they know it isn't an argument but rather a robust conversation. With the principle in mind, they hunt for reality. By focusing on the principle, and not personal attacks, a robust conversation becomes constructive.

If our company didn't develop a set of principles, we could fall for the tricks the business world serves up to leaders—money and power. Like any human, eventually we would be eaten by these two predators. Our principles give us something to stand for. We stand for something so we won't trip over everything. My hope and prayer is that our company identity does not evolve to an environment where stress-induced emergency room visits become commonplace.

ACTION ITEM:

Develop a set of principles that your company believes in and can stand on. Reference all the latest books you have read or workshops you have attended for help. One of the best starting points is the book of Proverbs.

PRAYER:

LORD, YOU ARE THE ULTIMATE SET OF PRINCIPLES.

TEACH ME THROUGH YOUR BOOK OF PROVERBS

WHAT IS TRUTH.

32

RAVING FANS

The oak leaves in my yard had buried my five-month-old, Lucy. Her three-year-old big sister, Noelle, bravely dug her out. In my defense, it was the end of the fall season and I wasn't the only one with a messy yard. I don't mind doing yard work, but the project was overwhelming and would require more time than baseball games, gymnastics, and church would allow this particular month. I needed landscaping services.

The first person scheduled to meet with me was supposed to show up on a Saturday. I rearranged a river trip to accommodate his busy schedule. He failed to show up. The second landscaper I called upon honored our meeting time and was a complete professional. He talked about his experience, his family, and was extremely patient with all our novice horticultural questions. My wife and I were excited to work with him. I waited a week for a quote and never received one. I called back, thinking, "Maybe I hadn't made myself clear." He apologized that he had been busy but would send a quote out the next day. He failed again. My expectations were not high. I just needed someone responsible who would do what he said he was going to do.

Having an identity is one thing, but actually living it out is another. Landscapers have "quality service" stuck on their trucks and other companies have mission statements on their websites. But businesspeople spend more time on the font and colors in their logo than implementing what they say they believe in. If the leader really believes in his identity and he aggressively drives it through the company, his customers will become raving fans.

Having raving fans as customers is an honor. Our company has a process to ensure our raving fans continue to participate in our growth. The raving-fan process has three components: (1) implement our identity (2) build relationships and (3) measure and monitor.

The first step of our raving-fan process is to implement our identity. We have created a set of belief systems and it is our company's job to act out these in every customer engagement. If I were to start a landscaping business, I believe that I would flourish if I implemented just one of our most sacred PAX Principles (the five habits to create raving fans):

1. **Do what you say you are going to do.**
2. **Say please and thank you.**
3. **Return phone calls and emails within twenty-four hours.**
4. **Show up on time.**
5. **Finish what you start.**

The second step of the raving-fan process requires us to build relationships with our customers. Implementing the above five habits attracts and retains business because the entrepreneur has displayed competency and integrity. But entrepreneurs want their customers excited! The enthusiasm happens in a collision of competency, integrity, and (very importantly) when **customers know that the people at the company personally like them.**

When customers know that they are liked, the company has satisfied a deep personal desire.

If the entrepreneur needs a kick starter to get the relationship going he should try asking a few important questions: To a fellow entrepreneur, "How did you start the business?" To a couple, "How did you meet? To others, "Where was your first job?" The conversation that follows is the starting point for a healthier long-term relationship between the company and the customer and ultimately, creates raving fans.

The third step of our raving-fan process is to measure and monitor. Warning: Now I'm going to get a little technical and geeky. Please engage the left side of your brain again. We put all of our customers into one of three buckets:

Accounts.

These are people not engaged in the culture. They don't buy multiple products; they don't show up at our educational or appreciation events. Frankly, they are difficult to reach by phone or email. Our company appreciates that they haven't left, but we would like to give them a better experience. The team has tried to reach out but usually the customer's life is so busy there is a real challenge to get deeper engagement.

Customers/Clients.

These are in-between customers. They are engaged, but only passively. They may own more than one product, however, they aren't screaming from the rooftops about their experience with the company. Sometimes it's because of their personality type, but at the end of the day, regardless of their personality, they are neither enthusiastic about the company, nor are they disappointed.

Raving Fans.

These customers love the company. How do we know? They told us in a survey. This survey is called the Net Promoter Score. It is one of the most efficient and widely used surveys by companies around the country. Once a year, the company simply emails its customers the one-question survey:

How likely are you to refer us to your friends and family?

The scale is from 0-10. The customer is a raving fan if they rated a nine or ten. (Read, *The Ultimate Question*, by Fred Reichheld to learn more.[32]) All companies love raving fans. Raving fans brag about the team. The entrepreneur can literally relax when he knows the customers are raving fans because he starts a conversation knowing they already like the company. They aren't raving fans just because they like coffee and friendly smiles. They are raving fans because somewhere along the way the team displayed competency and integrity. The company desire is to move all of the clients up the scoring system from accounts to raving fans. This drives business and referrals, and should be a key measurement of the company's success.

ACTION ITEM:

Implement a system to move clients into raving fans. Start by setting a company standard of doing what you say you are going to do.

PRAYER:

LORD, I DON'T EVEN LIKE SOME OF MY CUSTOMERS.

LOVE THEM THROUGH ME. I DON'T HAVE THE

CAPACITY TO LOVE THEM INDEPENDENTLY OF YOU.

33

ADVISORY COUNCIL

"Plans fail for lack of counsel, but with many advisers they succeed." — Proverbs 15:22 NIV

The entrepreneur has implemented his identity and because of his survey, he has a pulse of his customer sentiments. But he wants to dig deeper. He needs to know specifically what is working in this new company culture. To get this detailed information, he has to effectively engage customers and ask for feedback. Customers are the people who have the inside information and can shoot you straight. Unfortunately, it's scary asking customers. An entrepreneur gets nervous receiving critical client feedback because it pricks his pride. He may be reminded of the time his company messed up. But if a customer gives the feedback with a little love and the owner accepts it, that feedback is better than a pot of gold at the end of a rainbow.

The entrepreneur can hide his tail in-between his legs and hope he's doing all right. In that case, he might only have customers because they are too busy to consider alternative solutions. Without quality customer feedback, the entrepreneur goes with his gut and keeps assuming everyone is feeling good. You know what they say about the keepers of assumptions. Rather than assuming, our team turns to an advisory council.

An advisory council is a small group of five to ten customers who really believe in the business owner as a person and a leader. There are a few guidelines for selecting council members. First, they can't be the entrepreneur's family members. It would be too awkward around Thanksgiving dinner. Second, it benefits the entrepreneur when the customers own a business. It is not necessary to be a business owner to serve on the council but business owners' bonds are unique. Fellow entrepreneurs understand cash flow issues and the pressure that comes with owning a business.

For example, I received customer feedback from a non-entrepreneur customer requesting the elimination of our automated phone system. However, when I brought it up to my advisory council a different recommendation was given to me. Several of my advisory council members had been through the same cost evaluation process and they had decided it was too expensive to have someone answering the phone. The advisory council empathized with my desire to balance an awesome customer experience with managing cash flow. In the end, we agreed that it could be nice to have someone answering the phone all the time, but with limited cash, I had to be prudent and continue the use of the automated system.

The advisory council is anonymous to the community and agrees to keep conversations confidential. The entrepreneur needs to give the advisory council assurance of anonymity. This council must feel comfortable that they will not be in the newspaper if it is discovered that the entrepreneur has done something crooked.

The advisory council meets one or two times per year to get an update on the business plan and readdress the company mission and vision. The meeting is a half-day event and the agenda is extremely organized. Important people are contributing their time, and it should be honored. The entrepreneur shouldn't waste time with how much toilet paper to order unless he is stuck and can't figure out what to do after he's exhausted his own research. A small thank-you token for volunteering their time, like a leather folder or a gift basket, is a courteous way to honor the council members. The council members only serve for two years and then they are rotated out so the entrepreneur can get a fresh perspective.

Another use of the advisory council for the entrepreneur is to have them as a third-party to assist with any disputes that might arise between business partners. This is just a bonus; most of the focus of advisory council meetings will be on company strategy and ways to improve the client experience.

If the entrepreneur's next meeting is a few months away and he is struggling to pull the trigger on a decision, he can send a group email to the advisory council asking for feedback on how they would handle the situation if they were in his shoes. This type of email dialogue is extremely helpful to the entrepreneur when he is on the verge of an employee termination.

Many times, the members of the council will admit that they, too, were recipients of incredible business insight that will be implemented in their own companies. The advisory council is a creative way to get inside information from clients and, if their feedback is implemented, improves the client experience.

There are other organizations that provide this type of advisory council service for a monthly fee and a more frequent time commitment. There is nothing wrong with this approach. The C12 Group ™ is a national organization that has done an excellent job facilitating this type of program that stretches the entrepreneur.

ACTION ITEM:

Identify five people to be on your advisory council. Call them and let them know your intent and gauge their level of interest.

PRAYER:

LORD, YOU SAID THERE IS WISDOM IN THE COUNCIL

OF ADVISORS. GIVE ME DISCERNMENT TO KNOW WHO

TO REACH OUT TO.

34

ASSAULT ON BUSINESS IDENTITY

Godzilla confidently lowers his right foot on a building as he ventures toward the Statue of Liberty. People down below, looking like the size of ants, scatter in every direction. Godzilla turns his head and eyeballs airplanes and helicopters zooming toward him and spraying him with pellets that brush off his leathery skin. He feels no pain or fear. He lowers his left foot and levels a hotel. He moves more swiftly. He crushes a law office. He steps on a sandwich shop. He kicks over a hotdog stand. The street artists run away from their chalk. He's attacking America. He's annihilating businesses. But this Godzilla is not a giant lizard. This Godzilla represents a new anti-business belief system. The system is a subtle cultural issue. Unfortunately, America has come to believe that business is bad. The collective American vote is that money is bad. I believe this audacious claim (whether implied or explicit) is not just wrong but will crush us all.

We get indirect messages from Hollywood on a regular basis. They do a phenomenal job at exasperating the claim that business is bad. My son, Luke, who was six at the time, was quiet as he rode in the back of the car. We are comfortable just driving and not talking sometimes. Not because we don't get along, we just enjoy the quiet of not having four girls in the car singing *Frozen's* "Let it Go." Luke did, in a brief moment, let me in on his thoughts. "Dad, rich people are bad." "Really?" I asked. "What makes you think that?" "Well all the rich people in the movies are bad," he replied. I certainly didn't teach him bad and rich are associated. The assumption he made was that greed and selfishness are solely located in one demographic.

His comment made me think about the way I grew up and my childhood thoughts of the rich. Most of my extended family stretched their month until the end of the paycheck. I came from a culture that didn't get exposed to the rich on a regular basis. One man, Mr. Elliott, was someone I considered rich. His son and I became friends in high school. He was kind enough to invite me on several vacations with his family. Another man, Mr. Booker, was wealthy and he took me to a Spurs game as a child. My experience with the wealthy was minimal, but it wasn't bad. Given that I didn't watch a lot of movies or TV, I never hated the rich.

Not long after my son's insightful backseat comment, I was relaxing on the couch with my wife watching a Denzel Washington movie called *Unstoppable*. The basis of the movie is a train loaded with toxic materials on the move without any passengers, an engineer, or conductor. The throttle is stuck and the air brakes are disconnected forcing the train to speed through small towns and communities like a missile. A desperate team of people is working together to figure out a solution for stopping the train.

A call goes out to an executive of the company who owns the locomotive. The movie shows a middle-aged man puffing on a cigar while putting on the green of the ninth hole. The executive answers a call to his cell phone. On the other end is his management team surrounding a boardroom conference table with windows that overlook the city. The executive receives an update that the train is a danger to the lives of families across rural America. He is also told that the mistake could cost the company $100 million. With a golf club in hand, the executive asks, "And the resulting stock valuation?" "I project a thirty to forty percent devaluation," replied one of the members of the management team.[33] The implication is clear. The executive team was far more concerned about the company stock price than the lives in the small country towns.

This business-versus-the-people attitude portrayed by Hollywood is not uncommon. Assault on business doesn't just happen in the movies. It's on TV shows, on cartoons, in comedies, in politics, billboards, editorials, and blogs, and it becomes woven into the consciousness of the American culture. Today, we live in a culture that portrays business as inherently bad.

But, history tells us that business is good for families, communities, and God's work. My mom did a little research into our family history and I learned I had a strong Jewish lineage. When I have shared this fact with other people, I've been told that they weren't surprised because of how "thrifty" I can be. I mentioned this to one of my Jewish clients and he responded by saying, "Keep having kids because you'll never go broke!" I found out that I had a strong Jewish heritage and I was already being pigeonholed into Jewish stereotypes. That was quick.

I have always appreciated the Jewish community and have had a healthy desire to learn about their heritage and history. I love reading the Pentateuch and learning about the Apostle Paul. I have spent countless hours in Krav Maga training—the self-defense system required by all who have enlisted in the Israeli Armed Forces. In the midst of my studying and training, I've often wondered why the Jewish community is so financially prosperous. So I picked up a book by Rabbi Daniel Lapin called *Thou Shall Prosper*. In it, he discusses this topic. Do Jewish people cheat? Do they have a secret network? Are they smarter? No. Lapin said it is because the Jewish community believes a quest to pursue profit and wealth is inherently moral. There is nothing wrong with being rich! Business and money are long-held traditions that are good for the function of society.[34]

Do you remember the story of the Good Samaritan? The story is told in Luke 10:25-37. The Samaritan came across a bloodied man who had been beaten black-and-blue and left on the side of the road going from Jerusalem to Jericho. The Samaritan gave him a little water and the Jesus equivalent of Neosporin (oil and wine). The Samaritan put him in the backseat of his camel. He dropped him off at an inn. The Samaritan swiped his debit card at the front desk to ensure the poor man's recovery and a good night's rest. The Samaritan was able to accomplish one of the most generous acts of kindness in the history of mankind because he was a good steward of money and had the resources to help. Sure, there might have been others with money that were heartless and passed the guy by. Alternatively, there could have been people who wanted to help but didn't have any resources so they passed by as well. We don't know. What we do know is that someone with money was able and willing to help.

I realize some businesspeople are bad. However, the silent majority of entrepreneurs are not only resourceful, but thoughtful about their customers and employees. You see, business and money are not bad. The perception that "business is bad" is a Godzilla-like crisis and entrepreneurs must do their part to change this perception. What small business does is necessary for our nation and no one should be convinced differently.

ACTION ITEM:

Pay attention to the next sitcom or movie you watch and identify the subtle attacks on business.

PRAYER:

LORD, PLEASE TRANSFORM THE HEARTS AND

MINDS OF AMERICA. GIVE THEM AN AWARENESS OF

THE BENEFIT OF SMALL BUSINESS AND HOW IT IS

UNIQUELY QUALIFIED TO ACCOMPLISH YOUR WILL.

35

PROTECTING THE BUSINESS IDENTITY

How do we solve the Godzilla-like problem infecting our youth, culture, and future? I believe there are two stones we can sling at the giant's forehead.

The first solution is a small, flat stone, but an effective one—be a voice. There are organizations who advocate for business and especially small business. An entrepreneur needs to be active and participate locally in his chamber of commerce and nationally with the National Federation of Independent Business Owners (NFIB). Like breaking a pencil, individually, business owners are rarely heard. But collectively, they are powerful, like a handful of pencils which is nearly impossible to break with bare hands.

I know political involvement is a nuisance, but entrepreneurs need to chip in a little so their collective concerns are heard in their city, state, and country. Two-thirds of all jobs generated in the US are created by small businesses.[35] If our culture doesn't hear the cry and acknowledge entrepreneurs' collective impact, we're in trouble as a country. Jobs will be lost and families will suffer.

I was disappointed to hear from a business advocacy group about an attack that happened to a single-mom running her own photography business. She received a request to photograph an event that troubled her spirit. The photographer turned down the opportunity because it contradicted her value system. She recommended one of her peers instead and actually saved the customer money. She handled the situation extremely professionally. The customer was kind, understood, and even thankful for the recommendation. However, the state that this photographer conducted her business in was not pleased when they found out what had happened. Then, special interest groups joined in just to make this entrepreneur an example. Her freedom of commerce was crushed. I have not heard the end result of the litigation, but I'm not confident her business will survive.

Another example of an attack on business is one I personally participated in. I went up to the capitol of Texas with my pitchfork and decried that the state franchise tax imposed on small business was unjust. I wasn't yelling on my own. I united with many other business owners and our voices were heard. The outcome was that we significantly reduced the state franchise tax burden on thousands of small business owners allowing them to keep their money and use it where they feel it is best served. We wanted the tax eliminated, but the final outcome was still a success for many small business owners in the state.

The second solution is a big, round mini-boulder— look into the mirror. This stone is sure to draw blood from Godzilla's forehead. I reach into my PAX Principles toolbox for the rock. "When things go good we look out the window, but when things go bad we look in the mirror." Things are bad and they are getting worse, but entrepreneurs need to look in the mirror and recognize the damage they are inflicting themselves.

Business owners need to run their organizations with a high degree of integrity. Easy to do, but not done enough. It is in the one moment of the entrepreneur's life when he compromises his character that his reputation is crushed. Richard Nixon, an otherwise good president, will have more documentaries about how he cheated than how he led. Penn State head football coach, Joe Paterno, will not be remembered as one of the greatest coaches of all time, but rather a man who turned his back on the disgusting abuse of a child. General Petraeus, former director of the Central Intelligence Agency, betrayed his family and his commitment to marriage. My former mentor was generally a good guy but violated a few basic integrity laws and his reputation in the community will never be the same.

I'm going to go deep with you for a second. Follow me; I won't keep you there long. The entrepreneur knows, based on his personal history and the history of other successful intelligent leaders, he can't trust his own "self" to overcome a violation of integrity. It is just a matter of time before his "self" commits a transgression. The question is simple, to what degree will the future mistake cost him? Will it be fatal to his family or business?

How can he possibly work with a high degree of integrity when the books he reads are all about self? All the authors talk about is self-reliance, self-confidence, self-sufficiency, etc. All the experts say, "Look inside yourself." Isn't this the same "self" that caused a lot of good leaders to crumble? Self thoughts lead to a mind of selfishness. With this focus, entrepreneurs set themselves up for an identity that is centered on self, not on God.

ACTION ITEM:

The next time you read a self-help book, see if you recognize the pressure that the author puts on your "self" to get better.

PRAYER:

LORD, I CAN'T RUN THIS BUSINESS BY MY "SELF." I

NEED MORE THAN JUST YOUR "HELP." I NEED YOU.

36

MY IDENTITY ATTACK

One of the disadvantages of overcoming adversity is that the entrepreneur builds overconfidence in himself. He becomes the center of his business world. Eventually, this independent spirit will fail an entrepreneur. It will fail to give him the peace needed to steer clear of **pressure, worry, and the messy mind called confusion.** Sometime, in the middle of his business cycle, the entrepreneur may experience something similar to a heart attack—an identity attack.

I am not any different than most entrepreneurs. I built a track record that led me to believe I can accomplish anything with a little mental toughness and extra effort (MTXE). As I pushed through adversity I would reflect on my self-sufficiency motto—MTXE. I have never been inked with a tattoo but if I had, it would have said MTXE on my most sensitive body part (because I believed I was that tough). MTXE was the center of my identity. Unfortunately, the motto failed me. It failed my mind, body, business, and family.

I had left my corporate job and was working hard to get some momentum with my small business. The plaques sat in a drawer. Applause was a distant memory. It had been a few years since I received the last attaboy. Those attaboys combined with MTXE had always pushed me to the next level. Now they were gone.

My first identity attack happened to me physically. I had put part of my identity in sports and as I became older and less mobile, I experienced pain and discomfort. This is normal for anyone. But the person whose mind expects him to be seventeen and whose body doesn't cooperate experiences an uncomfortable transition. So, I decided to take up running. This sport appeared to be doable and with the introduction of MP3 players, I could work out and enjoy my love of music. Before an out-of-town business conference, I decided to go for a sunrise jog and enjoy the cool southern California breeze. Unfortunately, I got lost. The conference kicked off while horns honked at me as I jogged on the access road of the San Diego Freeway.

It was a frustrating experience but I didn't give up jogging. However, I just couldn't see myself becoming a marathon runner. Like any man who can't play football or basketball like they used to, I tried something else—golf. I put in countless hours at the driving range and took lessons. Unfortunately, despite my practice, I utterly embarrassed myself. I didn't just hit the ball badly; others felt badly for me. My athletic identity was attacked. I was trying in my own strength to find a way to overcome. Nothing was working.

Okay, so physical attacks can be overcome with a little perspective about how aging is a normal process. However, when physical attacks team up with mental attacks, the entrepreneur can get worn out. My mental attack was professional. After I returned home from the San Diego conference, I received a phone call from an angry client. He wasn't just angry, he was livid. I had made a clerical error that cost him $10,000. He was a big, bearded man with a closet full of guns. He wasn't going to mess around. He wanted it fixed, and he wanted it fixed now! I lost countless nights of sleep trying to figure out a solution. My professional identity was being attacked alongside my physical identity.

At this point, I was not enjoying myself; I was really messing things up. Still, I knew I was tough and could overcome this. A little MTXE and I could pull myself through. However, there was a straw climbing on the back of the camel. This time, my identity was being attacked through my family.

In this same season, my wife was expecting our third child, and she was eleven weeks into the pregnancy. To prevent further first trimester nausea, it was best for her not to travel in a car much so she decided to stay at home with our oldest child, Luke. I elected to go to the grocery store a few miles up the road with our then two-year-old daughter, Claire. We enjoyed the beautiful February weather as we drove down the four-lane suburban road in my little SUV. She smiled at her big girl one-on-one time with daddy.

The temperature was perfect. I call it "leather jacket and sunglasses weather." From the backseat, my daughter asked if she could roll her window down. I didn't hesitate to say, "Yes," and I rolled mine down as well. After a few minutes, her piercing scream penetrated my eardrums. The heel of her shoe had pressed the electronic button responsible for pushing the window up. Her tiny middle finger was wedged between the window and the door-frame. I quickly swerved and cut off the honking traffic to my right. I pulled in the McDonald's parking lot. I couldn't force the glass down using the driver's side button. I had limited options. I may need to punch and shatter the window to get her finger unstuck.

Fortunately, my daughter moved her foot and the window rolled down. Unfortunately, her finger was partially severed. As her finger was hanging on by skin, I raced to the hospital, less than one mile away. Blood covered her princess dress. We quickly settled into the emergency room and I made a call to my wife. She rushed to the hospital with Luke. After an overnight stay at the hospital, my daughter's finger reattached successfully, but not without pain and fear. The next evening after our daughter was released from the hospital, my wife lost the baby.

Life was out of control for me. The collective circumstances became more than just bad luck. It was very real. I didn't like how hollow I felt as a businessman, a father, or a person. My identity was being attacked from all sides.

It's a part of the journey; unfortunately, every entrepreneur will experience an identity attack. In one of three phases, he's either coming off an attack, in the middle of an attack, or about to experience one. It may be physical, professional, or family-related. Even worse, like me, it could be all three attacking at the same time.

ACTION ITEM:

Ask yourself, "Am I being attacked right now?" Is there something that is disturbing sleep?

_____

PRAYER:

LORD, I DRAW ON YOU FOR PEACE. I KNOW THAT

IDENTITY ATTACKS HAPPEN. I WANT TO BE WITH YOU

WHEN THEY DO.

DEPENDENCE

I needed answers. I knew a little about the Bible (probably just a little more than the average person). I believed in God. But, like any good Pharisee, I was quicker to point out someone else's problems than to examine my own life. Not knowing what book in the Bible I could turn to for help, I called a guy I knew, peripherally, named Bill Loveless. This man had a little gray hair and was familiar with the Bible. He had run a successful general contracting company and decided to walk away from it and go into full-time ministry. I wasn't sure why someone would do this, but he was clearly proud of what he was doing. His confidence was attractive because it didn't appear to be self-confidence. He carried himself well and walked humbly. I thought he might have some answers.

Over a cup of coffee and a few breakfast tacos, I shared my fears and concerns. Bill was slow to speak and quick to listen. He really didn't say a whole lot. I was impressed, because men are typically quick to offer solutions to problems and I don't think I would have responded well if he spewed out a bunch of advice. I don't remember exactly what he said, but I do remember what God said in the conversation through Bill. God wasn't audibly talking to me. There wasn't a verbal dialogue with the man in the sky. However, it was extremely clear that God used Bill to communicate something important to me. God asked me, "Are you done yet?"[36]

"Are you done trying to control your business? Are you done worrying about your future? Are you done trying to control your family? Are you done fretting? Are you done sweating? Are you done trying to be the center of your entrepreneurial world?"

"Are you done yet?"

Bill explained two scriptures I had heard before but that stood eighteen inches away from my heart, just hanging out in my head. The first verse is directly from the lips of Jesus. **"I am the vine, you are the branches. If you remain in me and I in you, you will bear much fruit; apart from me you can do nothing." (John 15:5)** I had to think long and hard about the last part of the verse "apart from me you can do nothing." At first glance, I had a hard time buying what Jesus was selling. There are plenty of people doing things without Christ. People have successful businesses, save the manatees, and score touchdowns without pointing their finger up in the air at God. But, ultimately, what Jesus is saying is that all those things and events are insignificant. Our souls will still be thirsty after the temporary sip of a successful event or closing a big deal. We will still feel the emptiness, longing for "something."

The second scripture Bill brought to my attention was **Galatians 5:22-23. Here, Paul says, "But the fruit of the Spirit is love, joy, peace, forbearance, kindness, goodness, faithfulness, gentleness, and self-control.** Against such things there is not law."

Paul tells us what exactly the soul longs for. He doesn't say life is all about the game-winning shot, closing the deal, getting an award or plaque, or meeting a sales goal. Paul tells us what Jesus means about bearing fruit, implying that the other euphoric highs are fruitless.

If the entrepreneur makes profit and money goals in life, he's not experiencing the fruit; he's just eating plastic grapes. What all men and women should strive to pursue is the fruit of the Spirit Paul tells us about. Go back to the John 15:5 scripture again. Jesus, said "... you will bear much fruit." In the original Greek text, bear means "to hold."[37] Think about it, the entrepreneur is not manufacturing fruit; he is just holding and experiencing the fruit by trusting in God. He enjoys fruit when he is dependent. He is living an abundant entrepreneurial life when God is in the center showering him with the fruit of the Spirit.

I continued to digest what Bill had told me and realized that experiencing fear is not a fruit. I saw that when I experienced patience, patience is a fruit. There was a direct connection between when I hung out with God and the resulting love and joy I experienced. I recognized that when I was intentional about having a relationship with my Heavenly Father, just like I would with my earthly father, I experienced a peace that can't be acquired with a debit card.

No wonder I felt so stressed out. I put myself in the center of my world. I was the center of my business and I was setting myself up for failure. I didn't experience the joy of a business owner. I was experiencing stress and anxiety. With a MTXE attitude, I could not overcome the attacks I was experiencing. My mind, body, and soul were working at a pace that would lead to a heart attack by age forty.

Bill challenged me to depend on Him (not Bill, but God). Not today, not tomorrow, not before I go to bed, not with a prayer before I eat dinner, not just when I wake up in the morning. He challenged me to depend on Him moment by moment. I accepted that challenge. I now know what entrepreneurial peace and joy are really like.

People come from all over the world to pursue the joy of the American Dream. I continue to personally hear and read many successful rags-to-riches stories. I love it! The entrepreneurial life is an awesome adventure. It is stimulating and addicting. As a small-business owner, you grow and stretch by overcoming adversity and flirting with the edge of disaster. You have the **unique character-building opportunity** few in the entire world get to participate in.

However, the price of the dream is steep. I'm not referring to the dollars or time invested. I am referring to the emotional commitment. You will drink gallons and gallons of worry, you will eat pounds of **pressure**, all the while trying to create order in your messy mind. You can't read enough self-help books to bring peace. Even if you implement half of the strategies discussed in this book, you will feel overwhelmed if it's done with a self-sufficient attitude.

In your next moment, in your next breath, you have two choices: you can continue to carry the burden of business or you can trust God. For my fellow business burden-carriers, I would like to ask you "Are you done yet?" If the answer is, "Yes," then the next moment is the beginning of a new entrepreneurial life ... and the next moment and the one after that. You have the incredible opportunity to trust God to carry the worry so you can live the unique entrepreneurial life you were called to live.

ACTION ITEM:

Read Galatians 5:22-23. Study it. Think about it. Memorize it. Are you experiencing some of the fruit?

PRAYER:

LORD, APART FROM YOU I CAN DO NOTHING. I

PLACE MY VISION, MY MONEY, MY PEOPLE, AND MY

IDENTITY IN YOUR HANDS. I COMMIT TO LIVING THE

ENTREPRENEURIAL LIFE IN MOMENT BY MOMENT

DEPENDENCE UPON YOU.

NOTES

1. ConocoPhillips Inc. Available at: http://www.answers.com/Q/what_is_ conocophillips_mission_statement. Accessed January 24, 2014
2. Nike, Inc. Available at: http://nikeinc.com/pages/about-nike-inc. Accessed January 24, 2014
3. Good Reads Home. Available at http://www.goodreads.com/quotes/476679-good-business-leaders-create-a-vision-articulate-the-vision-passionately Accessed January 24, 2014
4. ZD Net. Available at: http://www.zdnet.com/microsofts-new-mission-statement-no-more-computer-on-every-desk-7000021658/ Accessed January 24, 2014
5. Southwest Airlines. Available at: http://southwest.investorroom.com/ Accessed January 24, 2014
6. Biz Central. Available at: http://www.bizcentralusa.com/steps/pdf/Vision-Statement-Examples.pdf. Accessed January 24, 2014
7. Karrass, G. *Effective Negotiating: Strategies for Successful Negotiating.* Karrass; 1999
8. Zigler. Available at: http://www.ziglar.com/quotes/you-have-be-you-can-do. Accessed January 24, 2014
9. Marshall, R. "The Power of Purpose." Available at: http://thepowerofpurpose.org/. Accessed January 24, 2014
10. "The Daily Reckoning; An Independent Perspective on the Australian & Global Share Markets." Available at: http://www.dailyreckoning.com.au/elzeardbouffier/2007/02/19/. Accessed January 24, 2014
11. Carson, R. and Sanduski, S. *Tested in the Trenches: A 9-Step Plan for Building and Sustaining a Million Dollar Financial Services Practice.* Chicago, IL: Dearborn Trade Publishing; 2005. Stephen R. Covey Home. Available at: http//www.stephencovey.com/7habits/7habits.php. Accessed January 24, 2014
12. "Great Leaders Serve." Available at: http://greatleadersserve.org/for-yourleadership-tool-box-6-x-6/. Accessed January 24, 2014
13. Goodreads. Available at: http://www.goodreads.com/quotes/561272-business-is-all-about-solving-people-s-problems---at-a. Accessed January 24, 2014
14. Coonradt, C. *The Game of Work: How to Enjoy Work As Much As Play;* 3rd Edition. Park City, Utah: The Game of Work, Inc; 1997
15. Crabtree, G. *Simple Numbers, Straight Talk, Big Profits!* Huntsville: MJ Lane Publishing; 2011
16. Kiyosaki, C. *Rich Dad, Poor Dad: What the Rich Teach Their Kids about Money—That the Poor and the Middle Class Do Not.* New York: Hachette Digital, Inc; 2000
17. Ramsey, D. *Entreleadership: 20 Years of Practical Business Wisdom from the Trenches.* New York: Howard Books; 2011

18. BrainyQuote. Available at: http://www.brainyquote.com/quotes/quotes/e/errolflynn106803.html. Accessed January 24, 2014

19. Family Business Institute. Succession Planning. Available at http://www.familybusinessinstitute.com/index.php/Succession-Planning. Accessed February 16, 2014

20. Collins. Available at: http://www.jimcollins.com/media_topics/first-who.html. Accessed January 24, 2014

21. Disc Profile. Available at: https://www.discprofile.com/. Accessed January 24, 2014

22. IMDb. Available at: http://www.imdb.com/title/tt0349825/plotsummary?ref_=tt_stry_pl. Accessed January 24, 2014

23. BrainyQuotes. Available at: http://www.brainyquote.com/quotes/authors/p/pat_riley.html. Accessed January 24, 2014

24. Maxwell, J. *The 21 Irrefutable Laws of Leadership*. Georgia: Thomas Nelson Inc; 1998

25. Stephen R. Covey Home. Available at: http//www.stephencovey.com/7habits/7habits.php. Accessed January 24, 2014

26. Cundiff, M. Available at: http://www.markjcundiff.com/2013/05/12/henry-cloudchick-fil-a-leadercast/. Accessed January 24, 2014

27. Merriam-Webster. Available at: http://www.merriam-webster.com/dictionary/system. Accessed January 24, 2014

28. Merriam-Webster. Available at: http://www.merriam-webster.com/dictionary/identity. Accessed January 24, 2014

29. Bossidy L. Charan R. *Execution: The Discipline of Getting Things Done*. New York, NY: Crown Publishing Group; 2002

30. Dickson, J. *Humilitas: A Lost Key to Life, Love, and Leadership*. Grand Rapids, MI: Zondervan; 2011

31. Lencioni, P. *The Advantage: Why Organizational Health Trumps Everything Else in Business*. San Francisco, CA: Jossey-Bass; 2012

32. Reichheld, F. *The Ultimate Question: Driving Good Profits and True Growth*. Boston, MA: Harvard Business School Publishing Corporation; 2006

33. IMDb. Available at: http://www.imdb.com/title/tt0386588/. Accessed January 24, 2014

34. Lapin, D. *Thou Shall Prosper: Ten Commandments for Making Money*. Hoboken, JN: John Wiley & Sons, Inc.; 2002

35. SBA Office of Advocacy. Available at http://www.sba.gov/sites/default/files/sbfaq.pdf. Accessed January 24, 2014

36. Christ Is Life Ministries. Available at http://www.christislifeministries.com/. Accessed January 24, 2014

37. StudyLight.org. Available at http://www.studylight.org/lex/grk/gwview.cgi?n=3306. Accessed January 24, 2014